Oral Traditions

When Did the French Stop Speaking Latin?

Jana A. Brill

UNIVERSITY PRESS OF AMERICA,® INC.
Lanham • Boulder • New York • Toronto • Oxford

Copyright © 2006 by
University Press of America,® Inc.
4501 Forbes Boulevard
Suite 200
Lanham, Maryland 20706
UPA Acquisitions Department (301) 459-3366

PO Box 317
Oxford
OX2 9RU, UK

Library of Congress Control Number: 2005932580
ISBN 0-7618-3290-4 (paperback : alk. ppr.)

Contents

Preface

By the time the Latin-speaking soldiers of the Roman Empire were forced to leave Gaul in the 5th century A.D., the Celtic Language of the Gauls (Gaulish) had been replaced by a form of Latin (Gallo-Roman) "still very close to the forms of Latin spoken elsewhere in the dying Empire" (Rickard 15). The Franks were able to impose their name and rule on Gaul in the following century, but not their language. So Latin continued to be the language of "Francia." During centuries of reconstruction and innovation, however, it moved farther from its linguistic roots than any of the other versions spoken in the old Empire. The reasons for this are beyond the scope of this study, but certainly include such obvious conditions as the geographical distance from Rome, and the fiercely independent nature of the populace. By the 17th century it is agreed that classical French was established. In this study I propose the date of 1695 (only somewhat tongue in cheek) as the year the French stopped speaking Latin. This is the year of the first manuscript of Perrault's *Tales of Mother Goose*, and as this study will show, the exact linguistic moment when the "new" compound past was regularly assuming some of the expressive functions previously reserved for the simple form derived from Latin. The verb is the heart of the French sentence, and its shape has always reflected the state of the language as a whole.

Early Usage and Evolution of the Compound Past

Plautus is documented in the 2nd century B.C. using a compound (periphrastic) past tense with "habere" 'to have' following an adjectival past participle: "multa bona bene parta habemus" 'many good things well obtained we have' (Harris 1982 cited in Brill 1983: 7). Popular comedies of the era indicate that "the periphrastic perfect was probably a spoken as well as a written supplement to the perfect" (Brill 1983: 16). It has been suggested that in Low/ Vulgar Latin (the spoken Latin of the people, including Roman soldiers) the periphrastic perfect had replaced the classical perfect by the 3rd or 4th century A.D. By the 8th century A.D. the Proto-Romance of Gaul, Gallo-Roman, had "inherited from spoken Latin a fully grammaticized *periphrastic perfect*, whose function was to designate completed action with relevance to the speech act, and a *simple perfect*, derived by normal phonological evolution from the Latin perfect, whose function was that of an aorist, i.e. an event or an act which simply occurred in the past, with no other consideration involved" (Brill 1983: 16–17).

The continued evolution of this compound or periphrastic form involved not only the moving of the auxiliary to pre-position, but also moving other important grammatical information from suffix position (as in Latin) to pre-position. This was not an isolated incident of morphosyntactic shift. Just as some verbal inflections were replaced with auxiliaries, so were noun and pronoun declensions eventually replaced with articles, other pronouns, and prepositions. The moving of the verb "habere" to precede the past participle and the eventual addition of the second auxiliary "être" did not yet complete the development of this form. As long as direct object nouns and locational adverbs could interrupt the two parts of this compound (a position often called "mid-predicate"), it had to be considered periphrastic, and thus not fully grammaticized as a past tense that could rival the aorist function of the simple form in speech. It is generally argued that the new compound form remained periphrastic, what I have labelled PC′ (PC prime), throughout the middle ages. In 1695 Perrault made the conservative editorial decision to move the locational adverb *icy* from the "modern" post-PC position of the manuscript to the mid-predicate (and Latinate) position of the 1697 first edition. For Perrault, who was generally an advocate of the use of modern vernacular, this return to archaic literary elegance probably was meant to emphasize the distinction between the "oral language" of the fairy tale that he was editing, and the literary tale that he was creating. The very French compound past of the manuscript gives linguists the clue that this form had ceased being periphrastic in speech. It could be considered a full verb, and could rival the Latinate simple form in spoken French. The French were finally speaking French. The derivative or "simple" past did not just disappear of course, but continued to be used side by side with the compound form. It generally disappeared from speech entirely by the time of the French Revolution. It is said, however, that some pedantic professors, especially in the South of France, can be heard using it in lectures to this day. This simple past is of course still very important in written literary narratives and for certain other restricted functions such as reports of solemn events and the rapid-fire narrative of a newspaper sports report.

French medievalists and linguists have explained verb form choice in Old French (OF), that period generally referring to the mid 12th to mid 13th, centuries, as chaotic or arbitrary (Wartburg 1946:94; Sandmann: 1957: 290–92). We can say today that this chaos was the precursor to morphosyntactic shift and eventually change. Others have linked the distribution to assonance (Weinrich 1964: 242–3), position in a "laisse" (De Felice: 1957:37), semantic nuance (Yvon: 1964: 107–8), verse versus prose (Foulet 1920:272–5) or narration versus direct discourse (Weinrich 1964; Brill: 1983: 24). Eight hundred years later the change is here. The French no longer use the simple past in daily speech, instead they use the compound form.

I have selected passages from three texts representing different stages of development of the French language to illustrate the "before," "during," and "after" of this change in verb usage: *Aucassin et Nicolete*: 13th century confusion, free variation, and early stages of regular distribution; *Les Fées*: 17th century beginning of complementary distribution as the compound form switches from being only a PC′ to PC, and migrates from the stage to informal conversations in daily life; *Mémoires de la Reine Hortense*: 19th century preference for the new compound form in spoken French, with distinctions of style and register in the use of the simple form. The use of the "imparfait pittoresque" also called "l'imparfait de narration" as an alternative to the simple past in written narratives arises in this period (Rickard 142). I have attempted to find passages where one can hear the "voice" of the author, in the old philological sense. In the 13th century text that voice is a fairly educated scribe as he attempts to write down what he has heard in a tale, in the 17th century it is the voice of Charles Perrault writing the French version of an almost universal fairy tale, and in the 19th century the daughter of Josephine is writing her memoirs in very correct school-girl grammar. That is my method, to attempt to hear and describe how the language was once spoken, through texts that are of course written.

Table I: Abbreviations

C = conditional

CA = past conditional

FS = simple future

I = imperfect

IMP = imperative

IN = infinitive

INP = past infinitive

IS = imperfect subjunctive

P = present indicative

PA = past anterior

PC = compound past (Romance invention)

PC´ = periphrastic present perfect

PP = past participle

PPR = present participle

PQP = pluperfect

PS = simple past (derived from Latin)

S = present subjunctive

SP = past subjunctive

Chapter One

Aucassin et Nicolete

1. INTRODUCTION

Scholars agree that this tale of star-crossed love between a handsome young French noble and a beautiful young Spanish captive sold to a French Viscount by the Saracens (Arabs who invaded Europe and Africa in the Middle Ages) probably had its origins in Moorish Spain. It has been suggested that the Spanish cities of Valencia and Tarragona became Valence and Beaucaire (across the Rhône from Tarascon) in Provence, and that the Aucassin of the original was probably a Saracen. The original thus had more obvious religious as well as class distinctions bound up in the plot. The anonymous author, writing in a Franco-Picard dialect, used an unusual form which regularly alternated verse and prose. Medieval musical notation was provided for the verses which were meant to be sung.

There is only one known manuscript (No.2168 of the Bibliothèque Nationale in Paris). Fortunately, F. W. Bourdillon reproduced this MS in photo-facsimile and type-transliteration. Bourdillon numbered the lines (generally 37) in each column of the MS for easy reference. This was published in 1896 by Clarendon Press, London. In his 1919 edition Bourdillon footnotes any important changes from the original MS ("Anything of importance, however, is mentioned: xxxvii."), and carefully shows how the other major editions (Méon, Moland and d'Héricault, Gaston Paris, and Suchier) differ. These are primarily orthographic differences with some differences in interpretation of deciphering what the scribe had in mind. This edition shows division of the MS into 41 sections, alternating verse and prose (odd numbers are in verse, even are prose). The number of lines in each section varies from 10 (section 33) to 90 (section 24). Bourdillon also explains in great detail in his "Introduction" why Suchier's 1878 edition should be rejected by students and scholars. Based on his footnotes and comments, it is evident that Bourdillon's 1919 edition is closest to the original MS. Bourdillon notes no changes in verb morphosyntax, from the MS. With immense humility and gratitude for his meticulous definitive work, and that of his many respected colleagues, and having looked at his published reproduction, especially the type translit- eration which is so very useful, I have selected the 1919 Bourdillon edition as the basis for this study.

Although the compound and simple verb forms are found both in the verse and prose passages of this tale, it has been widely agreed and argued that verse is a less reliable indicator of general language use than prose. Not only does language evolve more slowly in verse than in prose, but the choice of a particular word or grammatical form is generally governed by the needs of the poetic form. Thus, the choice of simple versus compound verb form in the verse portions of this tale was probably based on the needs of meter or asso- nance. For example in Section 29:

En le canbre entre Aucassins,   (present)
(musical notes)
Li cortois et li gentis;
Il est venus dusque au lit,   (compound past)
Alec u li rois se gist;   (present)
Par devant lui s'arestit   (simple past)
Si parla, oés que dit: (simple past, imperative, simple past without s)

While it would be tempting to argue that the compound verb form in line 3 shows the beginnings of its usage for continued present relevance (he came and stayed there), it is more likely that the "u" of "venus" provided a good as- sonance to the "u" of the following word. Also, the 7-syllable line would have been one syllable short with a simple form, even with the pronunciation of the final syllable of "dusque." The study of assonances in particular and of other peculiarities of the verse portions has led Bourdillon and his colleagues to find that the language of these verses reflects an older state of Franco-Picard than the prose. He states in his Introduction: "The general turn of the verse parts is very archaic" (xxix). For the purposes of this discussion then, I will use only the prose portions of the text.

Weinrich argued persuasively that in this OF period one found the begin- nings of a narration versus discourse distribution of the two forms, the sim- ple form being found mainly in narration, and the compound form being used in discourse. By discourse he meant direct dialogue or conversation. The prose portions of this tale include both dialogue and narratives. In Brill (1983), to explain what seemed like exceptions to Weinrich's general theory of distribution as applied to *Aucassin et Nicolete*, I argued that in certain passages where the father was speaking directly to his son, the simple past intervened when he drifted off into narration in the middle of the conversation. Not all deviations from the general distribution can be explained in this way of course, however this is not an unusual conversational style and it is found still today. (When answering a direct question, my former father-in-law would often segue seamlessly into the narration of a movie plot or cartoon storyline.) In Chapter One, I argue, following Weinrich, that an emerging pattern of usage of the compound versus the simple past verb forms in the prose passages of this 13th century text can be related to a context of narration versus discourse. I will also examine patterns of verb form choice as a function of social class or education.

2. THE TALE AND THE GENRE

The story begins in the south of France with a confrontation between Aucassin and his father, the Count of Beaucaire. In humorous adolescent fashion, Aucassin proclaims that he will not go to war for his father, unless he can have the former Saracen captive, now the adopted daughter of a local Viscount, Nicolete, for himself. The count denies his request in typical paternal (and oral narrative) fashion by repeating the girl's history. He reminds his son (and the presumed audience) that she is/was a captive, that she had been brought from a distant land, that she was purchased from the Saracens by the Viscount of Beaucaire and brought to this town, that the Viscount has raised and baptized the girl and made her his daughter, and that one day he will give her in marriage to someone who will provide for her. The father makes it very clear that the match is unsuitable, but Aucassin persists and strikes a deal with his father: he will help his father fight his old enemy from Valence, if the father promises that he can at least be with Nicolete one time. In what most critics see as a parody of chivalry, the father forgets his promise, and the stage is thus set for the ensuing tangle of escapes and adventures, and the eventual and inevitable discovery that Nicolete is the long lost daughter of the King of Cartagena, and thus worthy of Aucassin. Indeed, as the hilarious parody of 13th century customs continues, she proves herself to be more worthy, noble, and heroic than he. The motif of role reversal is repeated throughout the tale, and is especially evident in the segment about the imaginary kingdom of Torelore, where men "give birth," and women go to war. The battle where apples, eggs, and rounds of cheese are hurled instead of lethal weapons is funny indeed, but it was no doubt also intended as a satire on the endless wars. And the audience must have been rolling in the dirt when Aucassin started singing a lovesick rendition of something like today's "Twinkle Twinkle Little Star."

(One hundred years ago however, Bourdillon interpreted this scene as charming instead of funny).

One can imagine the tale being told and retold throughout Spain and France in marketplaces, town squares and other public places where the common people gathered. It is not rendered in the polished language of the upper classes, although part of the fun of the tale is the different "levels" of language used by the various characters. The scribe often spelled the same word in different ways, generally an indication of a careless error committed in haste or uncertainty as to the appropriate spelling, or perhaps a clue to a different pronunciation. Such a transcription of an oral tale probably comes closest to representing the spoken language of this area. It has been argued by many experts that, judging by the language, the tale first arose in France near the end of the 12th century and beginning of the 13th. Scholars agree that the manuscript was created near the end of the 13th century. This puts the work squarely in what is traditionally referred to as Old French (OF), and in this case the Picard dialect. Although it is seen as unique in its genre of "cantefable," it has been linked to the "roman, conte, nouvelle, fabliau, or mime" (Linker v). It also shows elements of early puppet theatre, perhaps related to mime, and the type of "conte" often referred to today as folk or fairy tales.

3. CANTEFABLE AS FOLK OR FAIRY TALE OR FABLIAU

Many of the tropes of folk and fairy tales are found in our cantefable: a forest, potential beasts, Nicolete as a fairy with magical healing powers, a fountain as central to the action, a giant, a magical helper(s), the testing/maturing of the suitor, and of course the happy ending. No matter that the tale was originally Moorish, that Aucassin was originally a Muslim and thus the enemy, the standard folktale frame is all there: obstacle, quest, helper, resolution with good winning out over evil. One difference is that folk and fairy tales are generally serious and mysterious in tone and offer a moral in their ending, while this story is full of humor and clever wit, and there really seems to be no simple moral. Thus, although it resembles a fairy tale, it is not quite that.

The cantefable had the basic elements of a folktale, but the humor and wit of the "fabliaux." These witty "anecdotes" were very popular at the same time as our cantefable, and were also in verse. Unlike the folktale, and more like later puppet theater, their goal was to make people laugh, often through elaborate puns or linguistic misunderstandings, and always at the expense of others. There was generally just one plot. Their ribald humor targeted everyone: peasants, priests, cheating husbands and wives, the whole panoply of 12th to 14th century characters.

4. CANTEFABLE AS PRECURSOR TO PUPPET THEATER

The wandering minstrel/reciter of this 13th c. cantefable had much in common with the later European puppeteer. Both wandered the countryside in search of audiences, and both generally acted all or most of the parts. They were skilled in language and song, and they generally incorporated elements of the social causes of their day, openly or in veiled secretive language. However, whereas the story and the music of this cantefable were probably of Moorish origin, the puppeteer most likely owed his talent to the influence of Italy. French (and most European) puppet theater had its roots in the Italian Commedia dell'Arte. This type of street theater was a popular, inexpensive, and widespread form of entertainment in Europe in the late middle ages. Although comedy, farce and fairy tales were the staple repertoires, at various moments of political unrest, the characters could slyly transform a scene or a phrase into political or nationalist satire. The patriotic Czech puppeteer Jan Nepomucky Lastovka is famously remembered as provoking the Austrian occupiers of the late 1870's. When asked to perform in German, which he spoke fluently, his famous response was, "Yes, Commander, I speak German, but my actors don't" (Horejs 76). This witty reply was of course meant as an act of humorous defiance and cultural pride, but the Czechs also knew that the Austrians could not understand all of the political innuendo when the "puppets" spoke in Czech. Language choice, and choice of types of expression were integral parts of puppet theater. Likewise, when the herd boys in *Aucassin et Nicolete* refused to sing, but would tell the story of their meeting with Nicolete, they felt they were not betraying her confidence. The verses are widely accepted as the "secrets" of the story by most modern critics.

The French Guignol character was created by a former silk worker, turned dentist, in old Lyon around 1808. This was the time of the revival of the silk trade, almost wiped out by the anti-aristocratic Jacobins. Through the efforts of Napoléon, and the invention of the Jacquard loom, business was again flourishing. Guignol represented a "canut" or independent weaver. His costume was the simple monochrome garment of the working class. His dark features generally included a moustache with long, curled sides. This combination of oriental and Mediterranean traits reminded the audience that the silk trade came to Lyon from China via Italian merchants in the 1400's. It is in the role of popular hero, fighting injustice (the low wages of the canuts) with cleverly devised puns, metaphors, and humor, that Guignol shows a common heritage with our cantefable. While the tale of *Aucassin et Nicolete* was surely intended to entertain, the undercurrent of gallic wit and subtle satire of the ruling classes is evident. The Christian-Muslim conflict found in this cantefable was also replayed in later European puppet theatres. The brown-skinned

puppet with Arabic or Moorish features eventually came to represent such vil-
lains as the wicked landowner. And of course the devil puppet often showed
features such as an elongated nose and jet black hair and eyebrows. The
young Goethe was inspired by a very well-known German puppet play of his
day, *Dr. Faustus and the Dance of the Moors* (Purschke 8).

5. THE LANGUAGE OF THE TALE

One is always cautioned to avoid using medieval texts as models of grammar. In
the "Prefatory Note" to his 1919 edition Bourdillon states that this edition is
"rather more adapted for the reader who reads simply for pleasure. It is not intended to instruct in the rules of Old French grammar or the rudiments of Romance philology. To subject such a gem as *Aucassin et Nicolete* to such material
service would seem akin to cutting up the Kohinoor in order to make glazier's
diamonds" (vii). There are other reasons for avoiding grammatical analysis as
well. There is much free variation, misspelling, mixing of dialects, and general
mayhem with syntax. But in this case that is part of the point. From the confusion, one can see not only that the compound verb form is in general use at all
levels of speech, but also the beginnings of regularity in verb usage, especially
when the father speaks, and in the prose narratives. The language of this Picard
or Franco-Picard dialect of Arras is not very different from the eventual standard
that would later be referred to as Francien, although Bourdillon notes occasional
elements of German syntax, such as when the verb appears at the end:

> . . . por le castel deffendre (XVI)

6. THE LANGUAGE OF THE CHARACTERS

As in many a Shakespeare play, the characters in this tale have distinct language styles. I have commented on the verb form choice in a prose passage
for each character below, using the abbreviations noted in Table I.

My assumption is that as the tale was told and retold, the choice of verb
form was repeated in the same way. It became part of the story, just as in
France today where children's fairy tales are still generally recounted orally
and in written form in the simple past, and understood by children who have
not yet formally learned this form (see Appendix, transcription of recordings
of *Le Petit Chaperon Rouge*). Thus, despite the variation in the scribe's
spelling and occasional word omission or deletion, the verb forms were probably those that he had heard. Although this is therefore not spontaneous
speech, it does reflect the language in use at the time. As the verb forms and
other grammatical forms (e.g. section 24, Giant Herder "mellor" from Latin

"meliorem," modern French "meilleur") attest, this language was still fairly close syntactically and lexically to its Latin roots.

> *The Count: Aucassin's Father (section 2, lines 28–36)*
> ——Fix, *fait* li péres, ce ne *poroit* ester. Nicolete *laise*
> ester! Que ce *est* une caitive qui *fu amenée* d'estrange
> terre, si l'*acata* li visquens de ceste vile as Sarasins, si
> l'*amena* en ceste vile; si l'*a levée* et *bautisie* et *faite* sa
> fillole; si li *donra* un de ces jors un baceler qui du pain
> li *gaaignera* par honor. De ce n'*as* tu que faire. Et se
> tu fenme *vix* avoir, je te *donrai* le file a un roi u a un
> conte. Il n'*a* si rice home en France, se tu *vix* sa fille
> avoir, que tu ne l'*aies.*

The next to last paragraph of section 2 begins with the Count speaking directly to his son about the latter's wish to have Nicolete for himself. The verb sequence begins P, C, IMP, P, as the father explains that this would not be possible and that he should leave the issue alone. But then the Count drifts off into the third person narration of Nicolete's origins and her arrival in Beaucaire: PA, PS, PS. He then turns his attention back to his dialogue with his son and reminds him that the Viscount has raised this girl, baptized her, and adopted her as his daughter: PC′, PC′, PC′. This PC′ is the original use of the still new PC to show that what has happened is still in force at the moment of speech. He adds that the Viscount plans to give her away someday to a man who will provide for her with honor: FS, FS. He then tells his son that this is none of his business anyway and that he can marry the richest girl in France if he wants to: P, P, FS, P, P, S. This paragraph illustrates how my theory of an embedded narrative can support Weinrich's hypothesis of a narrative versus discourse distribution of the PS and PC. While all exceptions to Weinrich's hypothesis cannot be explained in this way (there is of course the general lack of uniformity of grammar in OF), the beginnings of a coherent narrative versus discourse distribution can be glimpsed in the father's speech.

> *The Viscount: Nicolete's Adopted Father (section 4, lines 10–16)*
> ——Sire, *fait* li visquens, ce *poise* moi qu'il i *va*, ne qu'il
> i *vient*, ne qu'il i *parole.* Je l'*avoie acatée* de mes deniers,
> si l'*avoie levée* et *bautisie* et *faite* ma filole; si li *donasse*
> un baceler qui du pain li *gaegnast* par honor. De ce n'*eüst*
> Aucassins vos fix que faire. Mais puis que vostre volentés
> *est* et vos bons, je l'*envoierai* en tel tere et en tel païs, que
> jamais ne le *verra* de ses ex.

The Viscount responds to the Count's wish to have Nicolete sent away. He begins by saying how much the idea pains him: P, P, P, P, P. He then retells the story of how Nicolete came to be purchased by him from the Saracens, and how he brought her to Beaucaire, raised her, baptized her, and made her his daughter. It is essentially the same recitation as that of the Count, but the Viscount uses the pluperfect instead of the past anterior and simple past: PQP, PQP, PQP, PQP. It is important to note that this "narrative" is in the first person, while the Count's narrative of these same events was in the third. As the PS began to lose ground to the compound forms, its use was eventually restricted to third person. Given the present point of reference of the Viscount's narrative (he starts off using P), one might have expected four PC´'s here. Without stretching too far to explain a grammatical irregularity it might be possible to suggest that the reciter and the scribe wanted to show that the Viscount, being of lesser status than the Count, was uncomfortable with the new PC´. With the PS no longer available for first person narratives, he settled on the slightly incorrect PQP, which nevertheless expressed anteriority. (I say "slightly" incorrect because the notion of grammatical "correctness" was probably not relevant or important in this genre and at that time.) The passage continues with three quaintly hypercorrect imperfect subjunctives in both the protasis and apodosis of his very polite conditional sentence: IS, IS, IS, where one can imagine the Viscount pulling himself up and proudly proclaiming that his intention "were to/would be to" give Nicolete to a young man who would provide for her honorably and that this would be none of Aucassin's business. The paragraph ends with P, FS, FS, as he capitulates to the Count and will send her away as the Count wishes. The imperfect subjunctive was still used in speech in this period (Rickard 62–63), but its use in the first person (e.g. "donasse" the first of the three IS) was on its way out. Although it has lingered to this day in third person narratives, like the PS, it is generally agreed that the IS had almost disappeared from the spoken language, along with the PS, by the end of the 17th century. In hypothetical sentences it was of course replaced by an I and a C, but the Viscount could just as easily have expressed his future plans in a less circuitous fashion using the FS, as did the Count. While the possibility exists that I am reading too much into this perfect little gem, this paragraph may serve to show how the minstrel/reciter and the scribe showed class distinction via language use.

Aucassin (section 10, lines 38–40)
———Pére, *fait* Aucassins, vesci vostre anemi qui tant vous *a gerroié* et mal *fait*! Vint ans (a) ja *dure* (duré) ceste gerre; onques ne *pot* iestre acievée par home.

Like his father, Aucassin shows use of the PC´ in direct discourse and PS for narration. In section 10 the narration serves to recall to the audience the father's promise. In lines 38–40 we have the verb sequence P, PC´, PC´, P (or PC´ depending on transcription), P. It is interesting to note however that the

PC′ are in the 3rd person singular ("Here is your enemy who has fought you so long and hurt you!") where PS could have been used. The PC is thus a PC′ in that Aucassin is emphasizing that this has happened and here he is! The notion of present relevance is strengthened by the use of P before and after the PC. If the character had just wanted to remind the audience of past events, the PS would have been the more usual form, especially with the 3rd person subject. The use of PC′ shows that not everyone had yet made the distinction that would be clarified in the next 400 years: the PC would be used to relate recent (eventually within 24 hours) past events, especially in first and second person accounts, while the PS was still necessary for remote past narration, especially in the 3rd person. (By the 19th century neither present relevance nor the passing of less than 24 hours were necessary to justify the use of a PC, it had become the default oral past for everyone. What eventually became the main distinguishing feature between PC and PS use was the type of discourse involved, as we shall see in Chapter Three). Also of interest in this passage is the not so subtle serious satire of war. Aucassin's character, for once not a buffoon, clearly states that no one seems able to stop this never-ending war. He attempts to make his father's enemy give his word that he will never again attack his father if he is set free, but, of course in this tale, the adults do not keep their word, as seen below.

> *(section 10, lines 45–53)*
> ——Ba! quex covens, biax fix?
> ——Avoi! pére, *avés* les vos *oblié(e)s?* Par mon cief, qui que les
> *oblit*, je nes *voil* mie oblier, ains me *tient* molt au cuer. Enne
> m'*eüstes* vos en covent que quant je *pris* les armes et j'*alai* a
> l'estor, que se Dix me *ramenoit* sain et sauf, que vos me *lairiés*
> Nicolete ma douce amie tant veïr que j'*aroie parlé* a li deus paroles
> ou trois, et que je l'*aroie* une fois *baisie* m'*eüstes* vos en covent,
> et ce *voil* je que vos me *tenés*!

In lines 46–53 of section 10 the tense sequence begins PC′, P, P, P. Aucassin asks his father if he has forgotten the promise and then tells him how this hurts him. The Latinate syntax which puts "les" after "avés" reinforces the early very expressive use of the PC′. He then launches into a narration that reminds the father of what he promised: PS, PS, PS, I, C, CA, CA, PS. These PS are the standard 3rd person accounts of past events. The hypothetical sequence I, C, CA, CA is also what would be correct even today. The passage ends with one more reminder of what was promised in the PS, and P, P to express that he expects the father to keep these promises now. All of this is what one might consider "correct" or appropriate verb usage, although the final P could have been an S.

(section 24, lines 37–40)
——Certes, *fait* Aucassins, je le vos *dirai* molt volentiers. Je *vig*
hui matin cacier en ceste forest, s'*avoie* un blanc levrier, le plus bel
del siecle, si *l'ai perdu*; por ce *pleur* jou.

In section 24 when Aucassin is speaking to the giant herder, his language
use seems less up to date. He agrees that he will tell (FS) the herder why he is
crying, but then uses a PS to explain that he came to the woods *that morning*
to hunt. Perhaps the PC with "être" as an auxiliary was considered too diffi-
cult or fancy for a conversation with a herder, but it would have definitely been
appropriate for two reasons: this was very recent, and it still had relevance—
he was still hunting. Many people continued to use the PS for events of the
same day in the 13th century, but I would venture that the more educated had
already started to use the PC for that purpose. We know that 400 years later
that change was complete. Aucassin then uses the PC´ to state that he has lost
his dog, an I to describe it, and concludes with a P to say that is why he is cry-
ing. The character of Aucassin seems a little confused as to when to use the
relatively new PC´. He seems to do better when talking to his father.

(section 40, lines 3–4)
——Biax dous amis, *fait* Aucassins, *savés* vos niënt de cele
Nicolete dont vos *avés* ci *canté?*

In this section Aucassin is addressing Nicolete who is disguised as a "jon-
gleur" or minstrel. The use of the locational adverb "ci" in mid-predicate position reinforces the periphrastic nature of the PC´.

The Narrator (section 16, lines 16–22)
Ele *segna* son cief , si se *laissa* glacier aval le fossé; et quant ele *vint*
u fons, si bel pié et ses beles mains, qui n'*avoient* mie *apris* c'on les
bleçast, furent quaissies et escorcies, et li sans en *sali* bien en doze
lius; et neporquant ele ne *santi* ne mal ne dolor por le grant paor qu'ele
avoit.

Section 16 is the account of Nicolete's escape from her tower. Beginning
with line 16, the narrator relates how she crossed (PS) herself and let herself
(PS) slide into the moat. When she came (PS) to the bottom, the narrator tells
us that her beautiful feet and hands which had not been accustomed (PQP) to
being hurt (IS) were (PS) bruised and torn. The use of the PS for 3rd singular past narration is very correct, as is the PS of "être" ("furent") or final I for
description. The IS in "qui n'avoient mie apris c'on les bleçast" 'that they be
hurt' was commonly used in speech but was not necessary here, after "apprendre que." This may prefigure modern usage of the subjunctive where it is

not needed, a situation that Rickard has referred to as "elegant variation" (143), but may in fact just be due to the confusion that has always surrounded use of the subjunctive.

> *(section 22, lines 1–4)*
> Quant Aucassins *oï* les pastoriax, si li *sovint* de
> Nicolete, se trés douce amie qu'il tant *amoit*, et si se
> *pensa* qu'ele *avoit* la *esté*. Et il *hurte* le ceval des
> esperons, si *vint* as pastoriax.

The narrator uses very appropriate PS to relate that when Aucassin heard the herd boys talking, he remembered Nicolete, whom he loved (I) so much, and so he thought (PS) that she had been (PQP) there. We must assume then that it was also very appropriate at the time to let the locational adverb "la" appear in mid-predicate position, thus reinforcing the periphrastic meaning of this PQP. The passage concludes with an historical P and a PS, as he spurs his horse and came to them.

> *The Wise Giant (section 24, lines 48–62)*
> ——Sire, je le vous *dirai*. J'*estoie* luiés a un rice vilain, si *caçoie*
> se carue; quatre bues i *avoit*. Or *a* trois jors qu'il m'*avint* une
> grande malaventure, que je *perdi* le mellor de mes bues, Roget,
> le mellor de me carue, si le *vois* querant. Si ne *mengai* ne ne
> *buç* trois jors *a* passés; si n'*os* aler a le vile, c'on me *metroit*
> en prison, que je ne l'*ai* de quoi saure. De tot l'avoir du monde
> *n'ai* je plus vaillant que vos *veés* sor le cors de mi. Une lasse
> mere *avoie*, si n'*avoit* plus vaillant que une keutisele, si li *a* on
> *sacie* de desous le dos, si *gist* a pur l'estrain; si m'en *poise* assés
> plus que de mi. Car avoirs *va* et *vient*; se j'*ai* or *perdu*, je
> *gaaignerai* une autre fois, si *sorrai* mon buef quant je *porrai*; ne
> ja por çou n'en *plouerai*. Et vos *plorastes* por un cien de longaigne!
> Mal dehait *ait* qui jamais vos *prisera*!

This section is one of the few in which the feudal system is overtly criticized in a serious rather than comic tone — except for the naming of the bull. The "giant" has lost an expensive bull, and is being asked by his master to pay for it. "20 sous" is serious money for a man who owns nothing more than the clothes on his back. He chastises Aucassin for crying about a lost dog (he takes this literally, although the audience knows this refers to Nicolete), while he is so poor that his mother's mattress was dragged from beneath her, presumably to pay his debts, yet he does not cry. The bed or mattress is traditionally the last item to go in folktales. (For example, in Jean Cocteau's classic film *Beauty and the Beast* the father can keep only his bed when his son bankrupts him).

It sounds like the minstrel/reciter changed to a serious voice to tell the giant's story. One presumes that there was just one performer playing all the parts, as in solo puppet theater. The giant uses both the PS and the PC´ to relate past events. He uses the PS to tell that he lost his bull "Roget" three days before and then didn't eat or drink. Since this is a first person direct discourse account, he could have used the new PC´, although the "past definite (PS) was normal in conversation with reference to the remote past" (Rickard 63). (Aucassin used the PS for telling he came to hunt that same morning!) The vivid scene of the mattress being dragged from beneath the mother is told in the PC´. Since this is in the third person 'one dragged the mattress from beneath my mother,' it would have been possible to use the traditional PS. Is the minstrel deliberately trying to signal that the giant is uneducated, because he uses a PS when he could have used a PC´ and vice versa, or is this just a good example of random verb use during this period? Of course the PC was created to show more vividly that an event had happened and its effects were still being felt—the mother now lies (P) on the floor. In the apodosis of a hypothesis, the herder uses a PC' instead of the later accepted P, followed by FS. This shows that the auxiliary "ai" 'have' in his PC´ still had the value of a full verb in the present, followed by an adjectival past participle (If I have money lost, I will earn it another time). This structure, interrupted by the object "or" 'gold' is somewhat old-fashioned, although still acceptable (Rickard 61). Likewise the giant alternates the more modern use of the possessive adjective "mes bues" 'my bull," with an older regional sounding periphrastic structure "le cors de mi" 'my body.'

The Talkative Herd Boy (section 22, line 6)
——Dix vos *benie*! *fait* cil qui *fu* plus enparlés des autres.

(section 22, lines 32–45)
——Sire, nos *estiiens* orains ci, entre prime et tierce (between 6 a.m.-9 a.m.), si *mangiëns* no pain a ceste fontaine, ausi con nos *faisons* ore; et une pucele *vint* ci, li plus bele riens du monde, si que nos *quidames* que ce *fust* une fée, et que tos cis bos en *esclarci*. Si nos *dona* tant del sien, que nos li *eümes* en covent, se vos *veniés* ci, nos vos *desisiens* que vos *alissiés* cacier en ceste forest; qu'il i *a* une beste que, se vos le *poiiés* prendre, vos n'en *donriiés* mie un des menbres por cinc cenz mars d'argent, ne por nul avoir; car li beste *a* tel mecine que, se vos le *poés* prendre, vos *serés* garis de vo mehaig; et dedens trios jors le vos *covient avoir prisse*, et se vos ne *l'avés prise*, jamais ne le *verrés*. Or le *caciés* se vos *volés* et se vos *volés* si le *laisciés*, car je m'en *sui* bien *acuités* vers li.

Some of the vocabulary (line 6 "benie" instead of "beneie") of the herd boy has been labeled "rustic" by Bourdillon (85 footnote). In this case the spelling is probably meant to be a clue to pronunciation. In the introduction to his edition Bourdillon noted that all three occurrences of the Picard variant for the first person plural imperfect: "estieens, mangiens, desisiens" were "possibly meant for rustic parlance" (xxxv). This background is instructive when we consider the uses of the PC and PS. The recitation of the herd boys' encounter with Nicolete that morning is told using a variety of I, PS, IS, P, C, FS, INP, PC´, IMP. The two PC´s come only towards the end when the talkative one stops the narration and tells Aucassin (in second person dialogue) that if "you have not taken" (PC´) the "beast" by the end of three days he will never see it again, and that it is up to him whether he hunts the "beast" or not, because (in first person dialogue) "I have fulfilled" (PC´) "my duty" in relaying Nicolete's message to him. This appears to suggest that although the least educated speakers of that time were already using the PC´ in dialogue, they were less likely to extend PC´ usage to third person narrative than their more educated counterparts. Aucassin also related events of the same day with a third person PS, but he then experimented with a PC´ in third person direct discourse with his father (section 10, line 38 above), even though he was referring to events of the distant past.

> *The King of Torelore (section 30, lines 5–6)*
> ——Ha! biax sire, *fait* li rois, que me *demandés* vos? *Avés* vos le sens
> *dervé*, qui en me maison me *batés*?

Lines 5 and 6 of the king's conversation with Aucassin show the interesting interruption of a PC by the direct object noun "le sens." This usage was also seen in the giant herder's line (section 24, line 59). It reinforces the early periphrastic function of the PC´ as an expression of completion or perfectivity, with continued present relevance. The interruption also reminds us that in the 13th century "avés" was still considered a full verb in the PC´ structure, not just an auxiliary.

> *Nicolete (section 16, lines 1–4)*
> ——Hé! *fait* Nicolete, l'ame de ten pére et de te mére *soit* en benooit
> repos, quant si belement et si cortoisement le m'*as* ore *dit*! Se Diu
> *plaist* je m'en *garderai* bien, et Dix m'en *gart!*

Nicolete does not have much of a voice in this tale. Most of her story is told by the narrator. Her longest speech is to the tower guard who warned her of danger. She thanks him using P, S, PC´, P, FS and IS. She is speaking directly to him and the PC´ refers to what he has just told her. It definitely has present relevance. The interesting syntax of the 13th century is: direct object, indirect object, auxiliary, conjunction/adverb, past participle ("le m'as ore dit"). Since she was the daughter of a king, her language was presumably meant to be elegant.

7. CONCLUSIONS

What have we "seen" and "heard" about 13th century verb usage from the characters of this tale? We know that the IS was widely used in speech by all levels of society, even when a subjunctive was not necessary. We know that the PS was still in common oral usage not only to narrate remote past events, but also to relate past actions of the same day and in the first or third person. The compound past was still a PC′ and was thus most often used when past events with present relevance were told to another person directly in a dialogue, that is it had not yet begun to seriously rival the PS in its aorist function. One of the most telling pieces of evidence of its continued periphrastic meaning is the use of direct object nouns as well as pronouns, and adverbs of location between an auxiliary and past participle, or mid-predicate position. It would not be until the late 17th century that nouns and locational adverbs ceased to divide the two parts of this verb form. Despite the contradictions and confusions, and given what we know today about the role of the PS in narration, Weinrich was probably correct in asserting that the primary distribution of PS/PC use was based on narration versus direct discourse. In addition there appeared to be a correlation between rustic speech, the use of elements of the Picard dialect, and the use of verb forms that most closely resembled their Latin counterparts: IS, PS. This could indicate that in this period the compound form was more readily adopted by the educated or literate, while others were more comfortable with the simple form, which ironically seems pedantic to us today.

BIBLIOGRAPHY

Bourdillon, F.W. *Cest Daucasì & De Nicolete: Photo-Facsimile and Type Transliteration from the Unique MS in the BN at Paris*. Oxford: Clarendon Press, 1896.
—— , ed. *Aucassin et Nicolete*. Manchester: University Press, 1919.
Brill, Jana A. *Past Times in French: A Study of the Passé Simple-Passé Composé Distribution, with Reference to Spanish and Italian*. Diss. University of California, Santa Barbara, 1983.
—— . "Determinative Adverb Syntax with French Compound Verb Forms." *French Review* 60, no.3 (February 1987): 359–65.
De Felice, Emilio. "Problemi di aspetto nei più antichi testi francesi." *Vox Romanica* 16 (1957): 1–51.
Foulet, Lucien. "La Disparition du prétérit." *Romania* 46 (1920): 271–313.
Harris, Martin. *The Evolution of French Syntax*. London: Longman, 1978.
—— . "The 'Past Simple' and the 'Present Perfect' in Romance." Pp.42–70 in *Studies in the Romance Verb*, edited by Nigel Vincent and Martin Harris. London: Croom Helm, 1982.

Horejs, Vìt, ed. *Czechoslovak-American Puppetry*. New York: GOH Productions/ Seven Loaves, Inc., 1994.

Purschke, Hans R. *The Puppet Theatre in Germany*. Darmstadt: Neue Darmstaedter Verlagsanstalt GmbH, 1957.

Rickard, Peter. *A History of the French Language*. London: Hutchinson University Library, 1974.

Sandmann, M. "Tempora des Erzählung im Altfranzösischen." *Vox Romanica* 16 (1957): 287–96.

Wartburg, Walter von. *Evolution et structure de la langue française*. 5th ed. Bern: Francke, 1946.

Weinrich, Harald. *Tempus*. Stuttgart: W. Kohlhammer GmbH, 1964.

Yvon, Henri. "Le Passé simple est-il en voie de disparition?" *Romania* 85 (1964): 101–11.

Chapter Two

Les Fées

1. INTRODUCTION

The face of Perrault scholarship changed in 1953 with the appearance of a manuscript "which had been discovered in Nice, was acquired by the [Pierpoint] Morgan Library, and made available to scholars" (Barchilon 16). This manuscript is dated 1695, and is titled *Contes de ma mère l'Oye* 'Tales of Mother Goose.' It contains "five of the eight stories" (Barchilon 18) that appeared two years later in the Barbin edition titled *Histoires ou contes du temps passé* 'Stories of Long Ago.' The existence of such a document had been hinted at by Perrault's relative, Mlle de l'Héritier, and by other contemporaries, but this was the first time modern scholars were able to view it.

In 1956 Barchilon published a reproduction of the manuscript along with an introduction and critical text. His discussion of the authorship and sources of the tales, as well as of Perrault's "textual improvements," is considered definitive by many in the field. He posits the existence of a (yet to be discovered) second manuscript that would show the changes Perrault made between 1695 and 1697. In any case, we have the first edition to show those changes. In Barchilon's critical text, footnotes to the reproduced manuscript show how the language was rewritten for the first edition. It was a footnote to the fifth tale, *Les Fées* 'The Fairies,' that contained the clue to a syntactic shift in progress. Barchilon (159) noted that the 1695 "est-ce que ie suis venue icy" had been changed to "Est-ce que je suis icy venue" for the 1697 first edition. This shift of the locational adverb "icy" to mid-predicate position is an important indicator of the status of the PC. For this reason, and because this tale was so carefully re-written by Perrault, and all agree that this re-writing was done by Charles not Pierre, that this tale came to represent for me the pivotal moment of a historic linguistic shift. Perrault was clearly correcting the oral

17

language of the manuscript in order to create his literary fairy tale. From a so-ciolinguistic point of view, one would say that this change in verb syntax had its origins in everyday speech (change from "below"). The new verb form had been finally embraced by the people, and this time the Academy was resist-ing its usage.

Barchilon mined this tale for other reasons. He wanted to establish author-ship. He painstakingly demonstrated how this tale was the most extensively re-written of the five in the manuscript. He found, in point by point comparisons of passages from the manuscript to the revisions for the first edition, evidence of the simple yet clear and detailed writing style of Charles Perrault. Thus, de-spite Pierre's signatures on the dedication and "privilèges" pages, and despite the statements of such contemporaries as Mlle l'Héritier and Mme Roche-Mazon, which supported the son as author, Barchilon's evidence weighs more in favor of Charles as the author. He wisely leaves open the possibility of col-laboration between father and son, and the possibility that Pierre dictated the tales he had heard from his father to the scribe. There is no doubt, however, that the revisions are the father's, for they are in his hand, and in his style.

2. TALE TYPE

Any analysis of a European folk or fairy tale must acknowledge the pioneer-ing work of such researchers as Aarne—Thompson (classification by type and motif), Bolte-Polívka (commentary to the Grimm collections), and later Propp (analysis by function of the characters). *Les Fées* is of course a fairy tale, one of the sub-categories of the folktale, and more specifically one vari-ant of what has been referred to as the "Cinderella Cycle." According to Propp, "All fairy tales, by their structure, belong to one and the same type" (21). Propp identifies thirty-one functions that can be found in a tale, not all of which need be present in each tale, but which must proceed in a set order. For this tale we note especially function #12—"The hero is tested in prepara-tion for receiving either a magical agent or helper" (Propp 36). Propp's ex-ample for this function applies directly to our story: "If the hero . . . answers rudely he receives nothing, but if he responds politely he is rewarded" (Propp 37). In Thompson's *Motif Index* (Thompson 424), it might belong in Chapter H under "Tests of Character." This type of analysis for classification purposes has been followed by countless others based on psychology and archetype (Jung), Marxist criticism, semiotics (Greimas, Courtès), structural anthropol-ogy (Lévi-Strauss), etc. The early works have nevertheless provided us with a common vocabulary. We now freely speak of "lack," "departure," "test," "(magical) agent," "donor," "reward," "punishment," etc.

There are countless variants of *The Fairies*. This is the story of a lovely mistreated daughter who through diligence and good manners finds diamonds, roses, pearls, and happiness with a prince. The unattractive lazy daughter finds toads, serpents, and death in her future. In the manuscript the sweet daughter resembles her gentle but dead mother, while the daughter of the new stepmother is loathsome in all ways. It is thought that Perrault modified this tale for the first edition so that it would not be so similar to "Cinderella" which was also included. Thus, in the first edition, it is the father who is dead and the lovely younger daughter resembles him. There is no remarriage, but the older daughter takes after her nasty mother in all ways. It is interesting that in both of these tales superficial looks correspond to character, a trope that is often the reverse in folktale tradition. In both versions there is a well, two fairies (really one in two disguises), and rewards or punishments that spew from the mouth. This delightful element reinforces the importance of speaking well and politely in French society. As an added twist, and test of the girls' character, the fairy that appears to the "good" girl is unattractive and old, while it is a young and beautiful princess that asks for water from the "bad" girl and is callously sent away to find her own. This subtlety is not present in the version published late in 1695 by Mlle l'Héritier, a relative of the Perrault family (Barchilon 51–55). In her version, the lovely girl is tempted by a lovely lady, and the unattractive girl is tempted by a fairy that resembles a peasant.

Although Zipes does not mention it specifically as a source in his 1992 study, *Les Fées* has much in common with Grimm's tale *Mother Holle*. In his 2001 book Zipes does include this tale, along with the Grimm's *Frau Holle*, Basile's *The Three Fairies*, L'Héritier's *The Enchantments of Eloquence; or, The Effects of Sweetness*, and Leprince de Beaumont's *Aurore and Aimée* in a chapter titled "Rewards and Punishments for Good and Bad Girls." Propp found similarities between *Frau Holle* and the Slavic tale *Morozko* (8), and so the common thread continued. In the mid-nineteenth century the Czechoslovak story teller Bozena Nemcovà called a similar tale *Sul nad zlato* 'salt over gold.' In this tale, a good and honest girl named Marushka (linguistically related to the name *Morozko*) is banished (and of course later rewarded) for telling her father that she loves him as much as salt. It takes the father some time (the whole length of the story of course) to understand how precious salt is.

By the time the Grimms began collecting their tales, many of Perrault's tales had spread throughout Europe and beyond. Although they may have had their sources in Italy or Greece, they had in turn become models for others. Zipes attributes "Mother Holle" to Dortchen Wild (1992, 730), the wife of Wilhelm Grimm. She in turn may have heard it from others in her circle of storytellers, including some who had French ancestry (Zipes 1992, xxiv).

The "Frenchness" of Perrault's version lies not only in its language, but in its social, geographical, and cultural setting. Thus we have the trope or motif of the well, the disguised fairy (possible Breton connection), and the very French insistence on the use of good language and polite manners. In the German *Mother Holle*, 160 years later, there is also a woman with two daughters, one good, one bad. There is also a clear reference to Perrault's work: "The other had to do all the housework and carry out the ashes like a Cinderella" (Zipes 1992, 96). There is also a well, and the good daughter falls into it as she seeks to retrieve a bloodied spindle or spool of yarn. In addition to the spinning motif, which is not present in Perrault's version, and the motif of retrieving a missing object (in *The Fairies* this could be the lack of water), there are added elements of a meadow, bread that needs to be removed from a baker's oven, an apple tree that needs shaking, an old woman with big teeth (a subtle reference to *Little Red Riding Hood*), and a feather bed that needed shaking, a symbol of winter not found in the Perrault tale. As a reward for her good work, the girl is covered in gold as she leaves Mother Holle's house. As in Perrault's tale, it is the mother who insists that the lazy daughter follow the path taken by the good girl. Of course the lazy one fails in all of the "tests" and is showered with pitch instead of gold. Feather beds are still very much a part of German and Slavic life, but this reference to winter was not as common in French tales. The various rewards of gold, jewels, and flowers are found in many of the precursor tales, as are the punishments with snakes and toads. The French tale emphasized the importance of speaking well and kindly, while the German tale emphasized the value of hard work. Despite the different settings and emphasis on different elements, they are basically the same tale.

3. PERRAULT'S VOICE(S)

Whose voice do we hear in the "Perrault" tales? Barchilon clearly believes that whether Pierre or Charles dictated to the scribe of the 1695 manuscript, there is ample evidence that Charles had told similar tales to his children, and that he had learned these from a variety of sources, including Straparola, the ladies of the court, and classic Greek mythology. The manuscript is believed to be more casual, more "oral," less clear, and less polished. Perhaps we can liken it to the odd hand-written draft that one occasionally still jots down today, before committing a text to the computer. The voice and the craft of Perrault are thus most visible in the text of the first edition, the one that is undisputedly his.

Barchilon carefully compares the language of the manuscript to the language of the first edition. He puts select passages side by side on his page which makes for easy comparison. In many cases the second is longer than the first. This is especially true in the passages selected for *Les Fées*. This is partially due to the changed storyline as noted above, but also because of the enhancements of style. "On several occasions Perrault interpolated a few significant words or even added a sentence in order to emphasize the drama or the humor in his stories. The effect of these interpolations is to the text what finishing touches are to a painting" (Barchilon 68). We know therefore that the text of the first edition represents the transformation of the rustic oral tale ("the sketch" of the manuscript) into a polished literary gem.

4. THE FRENCH ACADEMY

Perrault was inducted into the "Académie Française" at the age of 43, in 1671. According to Barchilon, it was Perrault "who initiated the custom of making a formal address to the Academy on election. This address has become an important tradition, and today every new member takes advantage of the occasion to praise his predecessor in a polished discourse" (Barchilon 102). This of course speaks to Perrault's great awareness of what would be considered polished French language at the close of the 17th century.

5. THE ROLE OF 17TH CENTURY FRENCH THEATRE

In 1565 the French grammarian Henri Estienne established a "24-hour rule" to distinguish the usage of the PC and the PS. This rule required the interval of one night to justify the use of the "distant" PS. This rule confounded 17th century dramatists, who were already laboring under the constraints of "the unities" of time, place, and action, and the "bienséances" 'rules of appropriate behaviour,' which often required *narration* of offstage events. Thus playwrights would be obliged to *narrate* an event of the same day using a PC. Corneille apparently refused repeatedly, and was reprimanded, as we know; but others obliged, or avoided the issue by using the imperfect and historical present. Thus, claims Weinrich (251), was born the modern tendency to narrate in the PC in certain media, such as letters, diaries, newspapers, theatre, and speech.

The 24-hour rule was doomed by its own precision. Linguists have shown many times, particularly in the case of American Indian languages, that it is a society's perception of time that is reflected in its language, and that this perception is by and large relative rather than absolute. Everyone's *day* did not start at the same hour, which led to confusion, in addition to rule-breaking.

There was also overt mockery in the mouths of Molière's servants, not of the rule but of those who subscribed to it in speech. Grammarians had by then modified the 24-hour rule, and suggested that the PS be reserved for a *more distant* past or a *historical past*, while the PC, in addition to being a perfect, would express any past with present relevance. Nevertheless, in the 17th century, the PS was in crisis. Even though narration of historical events was its assigned function, it was not used to narrate in such *oral* contexts as letters or diaries without the added semanteme or nuance of ostentation. Thus, an educated letter-writer such as Madame de Sévigné, anxious to follow the rules, would find herself in a dilemma when referring to an event that had occurred in a completely past time frame. She repeatedly states in her letters that she preferred a "natural" style, meaning that she wrote as she spoke, although her letters show more variation in style and tone than one would likely find in speech. Foulet points to numerous instances of one of her letters beginning with a PS (to satisfy the grammarians), then continuing in the PC, deemed more appropriate for an "oral" medium even for distant past events. In his 1945 *Introduction aux Lettres de Mme de Sévigné*, l'Abbé C. Hanlet cites this passage from a letter dated "27 mai 1680," where the shift from PS to PC is evident:

> Je *fus* hier au Buron, j'en *revins* le soir; je *pensai* pleurer en voyant
> la degradation de cette terre: il y *avait* les plus vieux bois du monde;
> mon fils, dans son dernier voyage, lui *a donné* les derniers coups de
> cognée. Il *a* encore *voulu* vendre un petit bouquet qui *faisait* une
> assez grande beauté; tout cela *est* pitoyable: il en *a rapporté* quatre
> cent pistoles dont il n'*eut* pas un sou un mois après.

The first and last PS could be attributed to the descriptive function often found at that time in parallel usage to the I. The PS of "revins," however, is clearly a nod to the 24-hour rule, especially in the context of the adverb "hier" 'yesterday.' This somewhat artificial problem was thus met with artificial solutions.

6. THE LANGUAGE OF THE TALE

The overall PS/PC distribution of this fairy tale reflects classic literary "written code." The PC has shed its periphrastic nuance in all but the one cited case, and is used only in quoted dialogue with a present point of reference. The PS serves as the main verb of past narration. Other verb forms in the narrative reinforce the atmosphere of timelessness inherent to the fairy tale:

Narrative Portions of the Tale

The Imperfect (I)

The tale begins, as many French tales do, with I:

(1) "Il *était* une fois. . ."

In the terminology of Limouzy et al, the aspect of this I would be described as "duratif statique," an ongoing state. Judge et al refer to it as the "aspect sé-cant," an action or state "seen as midstream" (94), and "seen from within" (105). It is also often referred to as "imperfective aspect." At a past point of reference, "somewhere in time" or "une fois," the most salient feature of this I is its aspect. Like the present, it represents a "nulltempus" (Blumenthal 122) or tense neutral verb. In describing the characters in the opening paragraph, it is telling us that there was no specific, or limiting, timeframe to this descrip-tion—no beginning, no endpoint—these characters were presumably always and forever thus: great archetypes suspended in time.

(2) ". . . que qui la *voyait voyait* la mère."

This iterative I could be read as "whenever anyone saw her they saw [in her] the mother." Thus we see an action or event repeated an undetermined num-ber of times, and with no specificity as to the duration of these encounters.

(3) "Il *fallait* entre autre chose. . ."

With this habitual/iterative I we are told of the many tasks that the younger daughter was required to perform, day after endless day.

(4) ". . . qui *revenait* de la chasse. . ."

Although in Judge's terminology "revenait" may be seen as expressing the "aspect sécant," in that it is durative, imperfective, and "seen from within," (not viewed from an outside point of view), in Limouzy's terminology it would be called "duratif dynamique" or "graduel." The latter term seems to best capture the notion of the prince riding along with no particular limiting timeframe, until the moment when he encounters the younger daughter cry-ing in the forest.

The Present (P)

(5) "Comme on *aime* naturellement son semblable. . ."

This is but one of several uses of P, a verb form that has been variously described as "tense neutral," and "encompassing a little bit of the future, and a little bit of the past." In its generic function of permanence or "eternal truth," "aime" tells us that loving one who resembles us is a trait inherent to humankind. Perrault added this observation on human nature to the first edition when he changed the opening set of characters. What the reader hears is that the mother, despite being the biological parent of both daughters, prefers the plain ill-mannered daughter, because she most resembles her, and that is as nature intended. Both the I and the P are aspectually imperfective: the former can be durative, progressive or graduel, iterative, or habitual; the latter is in this case permanent. The opening paragraph uses just these two verb forms, situating the tale "en dehors du temps" 'outside of time' (Limouzy 173).

The Simple Past (PS)

(6) "Le fils du Roi . . . la *rencontra*"

The arrival of the prince in (6) above is announced in the PS. This aspectually punctual verb form is the one most associated with the narrative portions of fairy tales, both because it advances the storyline, and because of its old world connotations, Even children *recognize*, but do not necessarily ever use, some of the most archaic forms of the PS. Even today, as it was three hundred years ago, the action of fairy tales and other children's stories unfolds primarily in the PS. While expressing past time, the PS reminds us that we are in the realm of timelessness.

The Pluperfect (PQP)

Augé writes that the PQP expresses "une chose passée relativement à une autre également passée" (231). There is no specific limit for time elapsed, just that one act must be anterior relative to the other. (This is where the PQP differs from the PA as we shall see below).

(7) ". . . car c'était une Fée qui *avait pris* la forme d'une pauvre femme du village."

(8) "La pauvre enfant lui raconta naïvement tout ce qui lui *était arrivé*."

Although the action of the PQP of (7) above seems less distant from its main verb than that of the PQP of (8), the verb form remains the same. For the PQP the criterion is simply anteriority, with no mention of a specific elapsed time.

The Past Anterior (PA)

(9) "Elle ne *fut* pas plus tôt *arrivée* à la fontaine qu'elle vit sortir. . ."

Like the PQP, the PA is temporally anterior to the verb of the main clause, in this case a PS. In addition to anteriority, the PA carries the aspectual message of immediacy. Augé writes that the PA expresses "qu'une chose a eu lieu immédiatement avant une autre" (231). This is generally true, and is true in (9), but is not necessarily always so (Judge 121). The adverbial conjunction "ne . . . pas plus tôt . . . que" is archaic, and would probably be replaced in modern French by "dès que" or "aussitôt que." Likewise, in modern French, the PA, which is often considered dated and pedantic or literary, is frequently avoided. Some modern alternatives to (9) above would be: "Etant arrivée, elle vit . . .," "Après être arrivée, elle vit . . .," "Aussitôt arrivée, elle vit. . ." In some regions of France (especially in the south), it might be rendered with a double compound past (passé surcomposé), thus emphasizing the aspectual notion of completion, while retaining the notion of anteriority: "Aussitôt qu'elle a été arrivée, elle a vu." Others would use instead a PC, with another PC in the main clause, thus neutralizing the aspectual immediacy and temporal anteriority of the message: "Aussitôt qu'elle est arrivée, elle a vu. . ." In some restricted cases (iterative aspect), a PQP can be used: "Aussitôt (chaque fois) qu'elle était arrivée, elle a vu. . ." In (9) above, we see the classic literary usage of the PA: "as soon as she had arrived at the well, the young daughter saw the disguised fairy. . ."

Subjunctive (S) and (IS), Infinitive (IN) and (INP), Present Participle (PPR)

(10a) ms. ". . . pour luy aider a *boire*. . ." (Barchilon 1956: 158). (no accents)
(10b) 1st ed. ". . . afin qu'elle *bût*. . ." (Barchilon 1956: 158 footnote to ms.).
(10c) 1981 ed. ". . . afin qu'elle *bût*. . ." (Collinet 1981: 165).

As previously discussed, it is clear to most literary historians that Charles Perrault prepared the final text for the first edition. Thus one finds in (10b, c) above, an elegant IS, where the ms. used the simpler IN. The IS construction was of course still common in the the 17th century, but its use today has been compared to being "roughly akin to an American speaking in iambic pentameter" (Bernstein cited in *Ouvertures*: 333). Most modern editors, including Collinet, have added accents, quotation marks, and hyphens, often missing in earlier editions.

The same pattern of a simpler verb form in the ms. as opposed to a more sophisticated and polished one in the first and later editions can be found in the examples below:

(11a) ms. ". . . *ayant eu* d'elle une fille toute semblable a sa mere. . ." (no accents)
(11b) 1st ed. ". . . estoit avec cela une des plus belles filles qu'on *eust sçeu* voir."
(11c) 1981 ed. "était avec cela une des plus belles filles qu'on *eût su* voir."

The phrase containing the participle construction of (11a) was replaced for the published edition with the phrase incorporating the highly sophisticated pluperfect subjunctive of (11b) and (11c). The compound PPR of (11a) expressed that the widower had a lovely daughter by his first wife. Her beauty is implied by the statement that she resembled her mother. The rephrasing of (11b) and (11c) states that the younger daughter (who resembled her father in this version) was the most beautiful girl that one had ever seen. The superlative and the need to express anteriority motivated the use of the pluperfect subjunctive. Today, a compound past subjunctive would be used, and probably without the verb "savoir," as in (11d) below:

(11d) ". . . qu'on *ait vu*."

The PPR is also used as a gerund, where it functions as an "adverbe de matière," and refers to the action of the subject of the main clause, as in (12) below:

(12) "Elle y alla, mais toujours en *grondant*."

The phrase expresses how the older daughter went to the well, grumbling the whole time.

The INP is often used in modern French to avoid use of the PA. It is also useful when one wishes to avoid repetition of the subject, as in "la malheureuse" of (13) below:

(13) ". . . et la malheureuse, après *avoir* bien *couru*. . ."

As the older daughter slithers off to die alone in the forest, this unpleasant girl, the only one in the tale to have a name, remains nameless.

The IN in (14) below is a most felicitous choice, especially in conjunction with "une infinité:"

(14) ". . .raconta . . . non sans *jeter* une infinité de Diamants. . ."

Since infinitives generally can only express aspect and voice, attention is focused on these. In the case of "jeter," the imperfective aspect stretches the timelessness of the act, so one is left with an image of never-ending riches, limited only perhaps by the time (not specified) it took the girl to finish her story.

The Conditional

The conditional in (15) below is modal:

(15) ". . . qui avait pris l'air et les habits d'une . . . pour voir jusqu'où *irait* la malhonnêteté. . ."

Like "au cas où," "jusqu'où" is a hypothetical conjunctive statement requiring the conditional. The point of view of the writer is that the older daughter is probably "malhonnête," it simply remains to be seen how rude or ill-mannered she is.

The archaic "voir" in (16) below is the emphatic equivalent of "vraiment:"

(16) ". . . Il me *ferait* beau voir, répondit la brutale, aller à la fontaine."

"Il me ferait beau voir" could be loosely translated as 'It would be totally useless," or "A lot of good it would do me." The older daughter is resisting her mother's request that she too should go to the well, in the hope of finding the same old woman who had previously bestowed riches on her sister. The modal conditional expresses an unlikely, contrary to reality concept.

Dialogue Portions of the Tale

The Present (P)

The P in (17) below, and others like it in the dialogue portion of the tale, refers to a state of affairs occurring at the moment of speech, with no set time limits. This imperfective state thus carries within it the shadow of the past and the hint of the future:

(17) "Vous *êtes* si belle, si bonne, et si honnête. . ."

Although it does connote timelessness, the P of (17) relates specifically to its subject "vous," unlike the P of (5) above, which expressed an eternal truth applicable to everyone.

The Simple Future (FS)

The simple future has also been called a "virtual" future (Blanche-Benveniste), in that it objectively makes a prediction, with no guarantees. There is an added nuance of timelessness to the prediction of (18) below, since the future acts will occur in an unspecified timeframe. Also, the second act depends on the completion of the first—if the girl decides to never speak again, nothing will come out of her mouth:

(18) ". . .qu'à chaque parole que vous *direz*, il vous *sortira* de la bouche. . ."

The FS contrasts to the compound future of modern spoken French, sometimes called the "immediate future," in that the latter is bound to the present moment, and expresses the speaker's "modal intention" to literally go and do something. This makes it seem that the action of the compound future is more likely to occur than that of a FS, but it does not necessarily mean more immediately, as many school textbooks imply. Judge (110) reminds us that both future forms can refer to such distant time frames as "l'année prochaine" 'next year,' and that FS phrases such as "j'irai tout de suite" 'I will go right away" are quite common. She prefers to describe the difference between the two forms ("if there is one") as "objective" (simple future) versus "subjective" (compound future). Whether it is viewed as objective or virtual, the FS of (18) above is both boundless and timeless. One does not know exactly when the events will occur or for how long this will go on once it starts. The reader presumes that once the girl begins to spout flowers and precious stones, it will be forever thus each time she speaks.

The Compound Past (PC)

The stage has now been set to examine the exceptional periphrastic PC´ in a dialogue portion of "Les Fées." From the previous explanations it is clear that the manuscript reflected more casual *oral* language, while the first edition became a polished *literary* text. As such, the latter reflected classic PS/PC distribution: the PS was used for the narration of events in a timeless past, and the PC was used in quoted dialogue with a present point of reference. Let us look again at the selected passage of dialogue:

ms. "est ce que ie suis venue icy"	'have I come here. . .'
1st ed. "Est-ce que je suis icy venue. . ."	'Am I here come. . .'

On the surface it may seem that the verb choice ("suis venue") in both examples is the same. However, because of the mid-predicate position of the adverb in the second phrase, we can conclude that this was the PC´, the older usage of the PC which echoed the Latin periphrasis, and implied not only that the action was recently accomplished, but that the auxiliary verb "suis" still retained some force as a full verb. The use of a PC´ also implies that the author wanted to emphasize aspectual completion. He could have resorted to the double compound form or "surcomposé," but according to Judge these double compound forms were ". . . eventually banned from written French as being clumsy" (100). There is still debate on the appropriate usage of these forms today, but most agree that their usage is restricted to the speech of various areas of the south. Cox adds ". . . most writers [today] avoid using [the double compound past], as if they were unwilling to believe their own ears" (698). Perrault's choice of the old PC´ for the first edition was subtle manipulation of the language in a way that would soon no longer be acceptable. The manuscript version reflected the way people actually *spoke* at the time. Whether the scribe was taking dictation from the father or the son, this is what he heard. The completely grammaticized PC with a locational adverb after the past participle indicated that this syntax had completed its journey from its Latin roots, at least in speech. This was a truly French, not a Latin construction.

In her letter of 1677, eighteen years before the Perrault manuscript, Mme de Sévigné showed the exact same syntax: "Je suis venue ici achever les beaux jours, et dire adieu aux feuilles; . . ." (Hanlet 53). The "French" usage was evidently already in use in "natural speech" well before my proposed date of 1695, but this date remains significant because for a famed academician the syntax was still negotiable.

7. CONCLUSIONS

The placement of adverbs in the French verb phrase has been the object of much linguistic study. It is generally agreed, however, that in modern French locational or "place" adverbs never interrupt compound verb forms (Ashby 81, Brill 1987). Although there was still some evidence of this as late as the 17th century, including the Perrault example, the language of the 17th century is widely considered to represent the beginning of "modern French." Unlike Aucassin who spoke in the PS with reference to an event of the same day, Perrault could not affect archaic erudition by using a PS in this example. (And in Aucassin's case this would have seemed rustic not erudite). The Perrault example is after all part of a conversation, and in the first person, and the rules forbade it, so he resorted to the subtle delights of syntax to create the desired effect. This would have been totally appropriate for a respected and important member of the French Academy.

BIBLIOGRAPHY

Ashby, William J. *Clitic Inflection in French: an historical perspective.* Amsterdam: Rodopi, 1977.

Augé, Claude. *Grammaire du certificat d'études.* Paris: Larousse, 1901.

Barchilon, Jacques. *Le Conte merveilleux français de 1690 à 1790: Cent ans de féerie et de poésie ignorée de l'histoire littéraire.* Paris: Champion, 1975.

———, *Perrrault's Tales of Mother Goose*: The Dedication Manuscript of 1695 reproduced in collotype facsimile with introduction and critical text. v.1. New York: The Pierpoint Morgan Library, 1956.

Bédier, Joseph. *Les fabliaux, études de littérature populaire et d'histoire littéraire du moyen-âge,* 5e éd. Paris: Librairie Ancienne Édouard Champion, 1925.

Bernstein, Richard. Excerpt from *Fragile Glory: A Portrait of France and the French.* P. 333 in *Ouvertures: Cours intermédiaire de français,* 2d ed. by H. Jay Siskin et al. Fort Worth: Holt, Rhinehart & Winston, 1998.

Blanche-Benveniste, Claire, and Colette Jeanjean. *Le Français parlé: transcription et édition.* Paris: Didier, 1987.

Blumenthal, Peter. *Vergangenheitstempora, Textstrukturierung und Zeitverständnis in der französischen Sprachgeschichte.* Stuttgart: Franz Steiner Verlag, 1986.

Bolte, J. and G. Polívka. *Anmerkungen zu den Kinder-und Hausmärchen der Brüder Grimm.* 5 Vols. Leipzig, 1913–31.

Brill, Jana A. "Past Times in French: A Study of the Passé Simple—Passé Composé Distribution, with Reference to Spanish and Italian." Diss. University of California, Santa Barbara, 1983.

———, "Determinative Adverb Syntax with French Compound Verb Forms." *French Review* 60, no. 3 (February 1987): 359–65. Courtès, J. *Introduction à la sémiotique narrative et discursive.* Paris: Hachette-Université, 1976.

Cox, Thomas J. Rev. of *Morphologie verbale et référence temporelle en français moderne,* by Hervé Curaat. *French Review* 66, no. 4 (March 1993): 698.

Delarue, Paul et Marie-Louise Ténèze. *Le conte populaire français: catalogue raisonée des versions de France.* Paris: Maisonneuve, 2002.

Foulet, Lucien. "La disparition du prétérit." *Romania* 46 (1920): 271–313.

Greimas, A. J. *Sémantique structurale.* Paris: Larousse, 1966.

Hanlet, l'Abbé C. *Introduction aux lettes de Mme de Sévigné.* Bruxelles: Anc. Établiss. J. Lebègue & Cie, 1945.

Judge, Anne, and F.G. Healey. *A Reference Grammar of Modern French.* London: Edward Arnold, 1985.

Jung, C. G. *Collected Works of C.G. Jung,* trans. R.F.C. Hull. Princeton: Princeton University Press, 1972.

Labov, William. *Sociolinguistic Patterns.* Philadelphia: U of Penn. Press, 1972.

Lévi-Strauss, Claude. *Structural Anthropology,* trans. Claire Jacobson and Brooke Schoeff. New York: Doubleday, 1963.

Limouzy, Pierre, and Jacques Bourgeacq. *Manuel de composition française,* 2d ed. New York: McGraw-Hill, 1990

Perrault, Charles. "Les Fées." *Contes,* ed. Jean-Pierre Collinet. Paris: Gallimard, 1981. 165–67.

Propp, Vladimir. *Morphology of the Folktale,* trans. Laurence Scott. 2d ed., 5th paperback printing. Austin: UT Press, 1975.

Thompson, Stith. *The Folktale.* New York: Dryden, 1946.

Zipes, Jack, trans. & introd. *The Complete Fairy Tales of the Brothers Grimm.* New York: Bantam Books, 1992.

Chapter Three

Mémoires de la Reine Hortense

1. INTRODUCTION

How do the memoirs of a 19th century queen fit into a volume which includes a satirical folk epic and a fairy tale? The heroines provide the first clue. At the beginning of their tales all three have lost their fathers. Nicolete has been kidnapped by Saracens in Spain and made a slave, the younger daughter resembles her dead father and is thus made to do the work of a household servant, and finally the noble father of Hortense is guillotined at the onset of the French Revolution. To be sure, the first two characters are fictional, but the story of Hortense also seems larger than life. She narrowly missed losing her mother to the guillotine as well, and it was of course through Josephine that Hortense eventually found wealth and prestige in Napoléon's court. The fictional Nicolete and the nameless younger daughter earned their fortunes through valor and kindness respectively. Hortense tried to make her reputation by being "good."

Secondly, each story comes to us first as an "oral" account that was then hand-written by a scribe or secretary. Hortense first jotted down some thoughts following the divorce of her mother from Napoléon I in 1809. Friends urged her to continue these notes as a memoir, but she felt that she did not have sufficient patience for such a task (Mém. 523). In 1812, Mme de Nansouty, a lady within her circle of friends, offered to write the memoirs for her if she dictated. The first effort was rejected immediately by Hortense: "Mais il y avait trop d'esprit: ce n'était pas moi" 'It was too clever: it wasn't me.' Like her 17th century predecessor, Mme de Sévigné, Hortense was determined to sound natural, to appear on paper as she appeared in her salons. This was a noble goal, but not an entirely attainable one, as we shall see below.

And so, in 1816, at the age of 33, Hortense began writing the memoirs herself. She composed this mixture of memories and opinions on everything from love to politics on loose four-sided stationary, some 550 pages in all. She made no divisions into chapters or volumes, this was done by subsequent editors. According to Jean Hanoteau, who had access to the archives when preparing his 1927 edition, these loose pages were mostly lost, but four manuscripts, copied by various members of her household remained. Hanoteau's notes to the 1927 edition explain how these documents passed from Hortense to her son Louis Napoléon (the future Napoléon III), then to his widow the Empress Eugénie, then to the Prince Napoléon (the younger son of King Jérôme), then to his widow Marie-Clotilde (S.A.I. la princesse Clotilde de Savoie, princesse Napoléon). It was the latter who made the complete archives, including letters from Napoléon I available to Hanoteau. Hortense would never know that her son would someday be president of France and emperor. When she died in 1837, she believed that basically everything had ended for her family. The "red" manuscript of 1820, copied by Mlle Courtin and bound in red Moroccan leather, is the basis of the 1927 edition. According to Hanoteau, the large margins show comments and revisions in the hand of Hortense as well as that of Mme Salvage, another in the circle of friends. Most page numbers in this study will refer to the red hardback version of the 1927 edition because it is the most complete. The pale green paperback edition, also of 1927, has more detailed notes however, and will therefore be cited as "Mém. P."

2. MEMOIRS AS AN ORAL GENRE

Memoirs are like letters to oneself, especially if there is no immediate intention to publish them. Hortense states at the outset that she is writing only for friends (Mém. 2). Indeed, many portions read like a young girl's diary. As it turned out, she later enjoyed reading these memoirs to friends in exile (Mém. P. xiv).

Scholars generally agree that the language of letters and diaries resembles that of spoken language. In 1974 Söll (27) specifically argued that these types of documents belong to what he labeled the "oral code." He listed the following features as belonging to the oral (versus written) code (Brill 1983: 111–12):

1. Use of the PC instead of the PS
2. Questions by rising intonation (infrequent in letters)
3. Use of "on" 'one' for "nous" 'we'
4. Use of "pas" for "ne . . . pas" (negative particles)

In addition, Söll-Hausmann suggested that letters require minimal preparation, that there is repetition of small vocabulary, that they are subjective, that the expression is longer and less profound than that of the written code, and that there are fewer adjectives and nouns—rather they are verb-oriented (63–65).

It is clear that the *Mémoires* belong neither entirely to the oral code nor the written. Only the first of the four specific features, listed by Söll-Hausmann applies, but that is the feature under consideration here. This feature and the secondary features of the oral code (repetition of small vocabulary, subjectivity, longer and less profound expression, verb-orientation) found in the writing of Hortense will be discussed in section four below. In the 17th century, as previously mentioned, Mme de Sévigné was required to begin her famous letters in the PS because of the constraints of the "24-hour rule." She then switched to the PC for recounting past actions because, it is assumed, that felt more appropriate to her in such an "oral" genre as letter-writing. By the time that Hortense began writing her memoirs in 1816 the rigid 24-hour rule had expired. A new distribution had taken its place for the written code: The PS would be used for entirely past events, especially historical notes, accounts of births, deaths, etc, while the PC would be used for past events that still had present relevance, or "whose effects could still be felt," as many grammarians put it. In the oral code there was only the PC. When there was doubt, there was always the picturesque imperfect or the historic present. The problem in the *Mémoires* is that Hortense frequently switched codes. As will be seen in section four below, her "narration" begins more as a conversation with the reader, in the PC. Although there are changes in code throughout, there seems to be an overall movement towards a more formal style, with a historical rather than a present point of reference, and thus a written code near the end. By 1820 the final installments show primarily the PS to express past events.

3. WHO WAS HORTENSE? HORTENSE IN HER OWN WORDS.

Hortense was the "younger" of two siblings, following her brother Eugène by two years. Alas, she had neither Josephines's looks nor her charm nor her cleverness. It would seem, reading between the lines as well as in certain self-aware passages, that much of her life was spent trying to earn her stepfather's love and esteem. Despite all of her apparent successes, however, Napoléon consistently considered her a child, as he did most women. Overall, one has the impression of a young woman trying to be virtuous, or at least to be useful, in a society where women were mostly considered mere ornaments.

The memoirs begin in June 1788. Hortense was a little more than five years old when she accompanied Josephine to visit her grandmother and their old homestead in Trois-Îlets, Martinique. Josephine had been born there on June 23, 1763, but this was Hortense's first visit. She had been born in Paris, the daughter of Josephine's first husband, Alexandre-François-Marie de Beauharnais, a nobleman who later died on the guillotine. Approximately thirty years later, Hortense recounts this visit to her parents' birthplace in the opening pages of her memoirs.

By some dictionary accounts, Josephine and de Beauharnais were "Créoles." Even though they were white plantation owners, at the time, this *noun* was applied to anyone born in the colonies. The *adjective* was reserved for the native population (Hoffmann 52–53). Hortense, however, was French and very proudly so, as her memoirs often reveal.

In the period leading up to the French Revolution, slavery in the colonies and the treatment of black slaves was very much an issue. The topic was hotly debated in political circles as well as literary salons. The most popular and politically correct view of the day was that slaves with good masters were happy. Slavery was considered an economic necessity for the success of the colonies.

Hortense opens her memoirs with the very vivid and precise memory of an encounter with her grandmother's slaves. This incident frames the memoirs, which then unfold as a long introspective lament. She sees herself throughout her life as a "slave" or "prisoner" of an arranged marriage, and as a provider of favors and pardons to the less fortunate. Her own "slavery" does not end until the Empire itself begins to unravel, and her husband (and uncle by marriage) Louis and stepfather Napoléon finally allow her a separation. As her memoirs come to a close, the black slave trade is abolished by France for the second and final time.

One can imagine the impact of this "framing" incident on her life. She was 35 years old when she wrote about this incident that had occurred when she was just 5. She appears to remember every vivid detail. She remembers playing near a table where her grandmother was counting money. Whenever a coin slipped, Hortense would run and retrieve it for her. When she saw her grandmother stack some large coins on a chair, and then leave the room, little Hortense somehow became convinced that this money was meant for her, to distribute to the poor slaves. She put the coins in the upturned hem of her dress, and then went to find the mulatto house servant Jean. Even at the age of 5, Hortense appeared to understand something of the social order of the colonies. Status was determined by skin color. Whites ruled, mulattos served inside the planters' homes, blacks worked outside on the plantations. Hortense apparently understood that she was not to contact the slaves directly. For this she needed Jean, who advised her on how to apportion the money. She instructed him to lead her to the slave quarters immediately, even though it was brutally hot under the midday sun. She proudly states that her mother's nurse received a double portion, and that when all the money was gone she was surrounded by blacks who were kissing her feet and hands. When she returned to the main house there was great turmoil. Her grandmother was look-ing for her money, and the poor servants were trembling in fear of being ac-cused. She immediately confessed to her grandmother, and the reprimand cost her a lifetime of regret and the lifelong need to make amends. She vowed never again to let her imagination carry her away (Mém. 4–5).

The grown Hortense continued to proclaim her innocence and the injustice of this and subsequent reprimands from various sources, including from her husband, from the emperor, from other powerful nobles and from court gos-sips who generally attributed more power and influence to her sundry schemes and ideas than she ever actually had.

What had fed the five-year-old's "imagination?" What might she have seen and heard from Josephine and her friends? Talk of slaves and slavery, the status of blacks versus mulattos, tales of slave revolts, good versus bad masters, surely some of this had reached her little girl ears. How did a five-year-old know to give a command to a house servant, and expect to be obeyed, even in the searing sun?

According to Hoffmann in his 1973 work *Le Nègre Romantique* 'The Ro-mantic [Literary] Negro,' "Pre-revolutionary life in the colonies, as repre-sented by men of letters, unfolded outside of time and in the margins of his-tory. Only the existence of slavery made it problematic. And even so, slavery was often just a picturesque footnote; much like the palm trees and the sugar plantations, it was part of the stock image of the exotic life in the Antilles" (101). Like the sugar plantations and the palm trees, the people of the islands had been stereotyped in the minds of the French back home. Common themes in the Paris salons as well as in the theaters were: the good master with the virtuous slaves versus the bad plantation owner with black victims; the gen-erous African prince versus the treacherous slave trader, who was of course either Spanish or English (Hoffmann 101). Even as a five-year-old, Hortense must have seen her grandmother as one of the "good masters," and as an ex-tension of that image, she considered herself "a good little mistress" as she distributed her coins. Also, she must have somehow understood in her young mind, probably from watching her grandmother, that she should not go to the slave quarters directly herself, but that she should summon the mulatto house servant for assistance. "Pigmentation defined social class" (Hoffmann 52).

The Revolution changed everything of course. "The tyranny of the coloniz-ers was associated with that of the privileged classes and bloodthirsty royalty:"

> . . . la cause du peuple, qui assimile la tyrannie des colons à celle des privilégiés et des rois assoiffés de sang. (Hoffmann 102).

"Roles were suddenly reversed: Colonizers became victims, and Blacks be-came the oppressors:"

> Les roles semblent soudain renversés: les colons deviennent des victims,
> ce sont les Noirs qui deviennent les bourreaux (Hoffmann 102).

Hortense and Josephine found themselves on the run in Martinique, as townspeople fired on the boat in which they had taken refuge. It was September 4, 1790, and "the Revolution had come to the islands" (Mém. P. 8). This sudden and dangerous departure from Martinique was documented thirty years later, but still with the mind of a child. The point of view was entirely that of someone concerned only for her own and her mother's safety. It was not until they arrived in Toulon in November of that same year, that Josephine learned of the specifics of the Revolution. Reunited with her nine-year-old brother Eugène, Hortense focuses entirely on retelling the story of their escape from Martinique under fire, and on relating the episode where her brother's tutor, an abbot, was seized by a revolutionary mob, was harnassed and made to pull a buggy. She excuses herself as "too young to understand what was happening around her" (Mém. 6). And so, her memoirs continue as a child-centered view of revolutionary events, with very little commentary or insight by their 37-year-old author.

Philology attempts to find "something of the tone, the living voice" (Clausen 15 in Ziolkowski). And that is what I was listening for as I read these memoirs. When children of nobles were required to learn a trade, Hortense recalls the little gifts given to Eugène by the sisters of his carpenter teacher. Again, there is very little appreciation of the social implication of this event. Her memory of the required outdoor communal supper in 1793 remains equally superficial. She remembers everyone who sat at her table, and that her mother could not attend because she, along with their American house guests, was in jail. Her building was thus represented by Josephine's servant Gonthier, their chamber maid Agathe, the porter and his wife, Hortense's governess Mlle de Lannoy, Hortense, and Eugène. She recalls not the importance of community, but that the governess was indignant at having to sit with the servants. She also recalls that passersby insulted them by calling them "aristocrats," and by insisting that their table was too close to their door. They immediately moved it to the middle of the street with the others. After dinner, Hortense remembers going around to other neighborhoods where the dinners were more festive (presumably because no one was in jail), and where the tables were more decorated.

Throughout the Terror Hortense maintained her constant love of France, and made much of trying to be virtuous and "good." She described the guillotine, the death of her father, and her very brief version of Josephine's narrow escape (she fainted, her execution was delayed, and the next day the Terror was over), in about as many pages as the rose prize she won for good character at school (Mém. 25–26). This prize was very competitive and little Hortense was determined to win it. The memoirs state that she remained quiet when it was announced that the prize would be shared by Hortense and her cousin Émilie, but the sound you hear between the lines is the great need of this former distributor of her grandmother's coins to be judged "good." She needed her "good character" officially certified in order to undo the mental damage done by her grandmother's rebuke. She needed full vindication, and only received half.

The Consulate and the Empire brought new opportunities for the still young Hortense to engage in good works. She undertook the tutoring of Napoléon's sister Caroline, who was not able to read at the age of 16. She nursed her mother back to health after a fall. After seeing how Josephine interceded on behalf of noble émigrés, Hortense seemed to find a new calling. She would do "good" on behalf of others. At 17 she writes, "I had the happiness of pleasing everyone" (Mém. 38). She claims to have had an influence in keeping the peace between Napoléon's warring generals (Mém. 46), and on their love lives (Mém. 49). She was still hoping for a perfect love match for herself, but instead she submitted to the marriage that Napoléon had arranged for her with his brother Louis. Her only protest was to insist on dressing simply, since she was not in love (Mém. 65).

Hortense soon found herself in the impossible position of not being able to please both her mother and her husband. When Josephine required her presence, Louis forbade her leaving him. Napoléon finally proclaimed that "a woman with as spotless a reputation as yours has the right to speak forcefully and should not be subject to ridiculous obligations" (Mém. 81). Hortense then understood that she had committed another fault—indiscretion. Her main flaw, however, seems to have been the total abdication of her own will. In an effort to please others, she had turned her own life into a prison. This is a flaw that even the older Hortense did not see. She saw herself as a victim. To cope, perhaps to compensate, and perhaps to elevate this flaw to a virtue, she became a "mother figure" for other young women in her entourage. When one appeared to be too flirtatious at a ball, "I spoke to her about her duties to her husband, and she listened to my advice as to a mother" (Mém. 82).

Hortense often speaks proudly about giving advice to Napoléon. And she did manage to have several death sentences commuted. She admits, however, to a specific incident when after listening to both Joséphine and Hortense, Napoléon took Joséphine into his arms and stated: "You are children" (Mém.84). This is probably the most accurate description of how both Napoléon and Louis viewed their wives. They were generally treated as children. Napoléon saw to every detail of their existence. He even appointed their personal household staff. Hortense especially had no real role as "Queen of

Holland" when Louis became king. Unlike Napoléon, who treated Joséphine with love and respect, Louis belittled and ridiculed Hortense publicly. He dictated who would attend her during childbirth, and where it would take place. He decided that she would not be allowed to nurse. Napoléon chose her card partners (for political reasons), named her children and wanted to adopt at least one of them, hoping that this would satisfy his people's need for an heir. At about this time (1805–1806), Hortense began reflecting on the nature of a woman's suffering. She was suffocating in her marriage. In her memoirs she recalls thinking of a fairy tale from her childhood in which an estranged mother takes on the post of governess to her children so that she could be near them: "I was convinced that this mother's fate was to be mine, and by accepting the throne [of Holland] I believed I was entering into slavery" (Mém. 140).

Hortense does, however, manage to "escape" from her husband/master periodically. She quite melodramatically proclaims that the three days she enjoyed with her children on a boat trip down the Rhine were "three happy days in my life" (Mém. 148). She was implying of course that these had been the only three happy days of her life. When Louis demanded her [marital] affection in a written document with "8 Articles," Hortense demanded kindness first. And so, the stalemate in their marriage continued, and Hortense continued in her role of suffering heroine. After the death of her son from croup in 1807, Hortense prefigures the Romantics in lamenting that nature was not in harmony with the state of her soul: "This enchanting valley [in the Pyrenees] did not reflect the disposition of my soul. I needed that severe countryside appropriate to profound sadness, because it is in harmony with it" (Mém. 171).

A linguistic note provides further insights into the cruelty of this marriage. Louis wanted Hortense to stop using the informal "tu" 'you' to her school friends. He claimed that it was to set an "example of all virtues" (Mém. 175) to these young ladies. But this was obviously another effort to control her every move, her every word. Even today, even in the most formal settings, one is allowed to use "tu" to old school chums. By coupling this request with an order to never receive anyone in her private quarters, Louis was enforcing linguistic and physical distance from those that cared about her. It would not be totally inappropriate to hypothesize that the increasing formality in tone of the memoirs is linked to the increasing formality in her household. Louis and Hortense always used the formal "vous" 'you' (Mém. 71) to each other, not uncommon for royalty, but nevertheless an indication of formality in the relationship.

Hortense's preoccupation with childish distractions and court liaisons was not entirely her fault. She admits in her memoirs of 1808 (age 25): "I was totally unaware of world events and the Emperor enjoyed keeping us in this state of ignorance, even when it concerned us personally. I only learned of the appointment of my elder son as Grand Duke of Berg when the 'master of ceremonies' wrote to my lady-in-waiting asking when I would be available to receive the compliments of the Senate" (Mém. 215).

Finally, after Louis abdicated the throne of Holland, Hortense was allowed to separate from him. She paid his debts (from her own allowance) and then returned to Paris in 1810 as a French princess. For the first time in her life (at age 27), she became the mistress of her own house, and was able to "arrange her life according to her own tastes" (Mém. 270). It is interesting to note, however, that her days were spent in much the same patterns as before: "drawing lessons, receiving visitors with her children, music, billiards, tea" (Mém.271). One big difference was that she no longer needed permission to visit Joséphine at Malmaison. Her good friend Mme de Broc encouraged her to be happy, despite the unhappiness of her marriage: "After such a long period of slavery, you are finally free, mistress of your own actions. You have your children close to you, an immense fortune, and the capacity to do good works. You are loved and esteemed by those who know you. Stop complaining about your fate!" (Mém.274). And so, Hortense plunged into charity work. Her virtue finally certified and rewarded, she continued to do good works. She took charge of 600 of Napoléon's war orphans at Saint-Denis and Écouen. When the European Coalition attacked Paris in 1814, Hortense stayed until the end. She finally had the courage to defy Louis, who wanted her to flee with him to safety. She refused: "The idea of becoming a prisoner of war seemed hardly as cruel as returning to a man who had spread so much bitterness on my life. He seemed to be waiting for this moment to retake his prey" (Mém. 321–22). When Louis ordered her to follow the Empress Marie-Louise [to Austria], Hortense fled instead to Navarre to join her mother. One humorous note to this escape, Hortense alone had thought to bring along a map of the Paris suburbs, so that she and her entourage could find a way around the advancing Cosacks. Having no more income and no more titles, she now dreams of returning to Martinique, a free woman. She does have her "diamonds" to sustain her and her children, but she delights in telling them that they are no longer royals. "At the approach of the enemy, in order for them to share in the country's misfortune, she cuts out dessert from their dinner, and they accepted this privation with joy" (Mém. 328).

Although she would revel in the brief return of Napoléon from Elbe, Hortense was never to know that her youngest son would one day be crowned Napoléon III. She died in 1837 at the age of 54, ever virtuous, obedient, patriotic, and a bit overly preoccupied with her role as tragic heroine. She had seen herself as a "slave" of her marriage. But the word was as romanticized as the condition of slavery itself had been. The only time that Hortense had truly approached the slave experience was when she and her mother were fleeing for their lives from Martinique, at the onset of the Revolution.

4. THE LANGUAGE OF THE MÉMOIRES

There have always been two French languages: the spoken (oral code), and the written. Hortense was writing for her friends, as we know. She thus began in what has been called the "oral code" of conversation, letters, journals, etc. This is in contrast to the beginnings of letters by the 17th century writer Mme de Sévigné, who, as we have seen, began her letters with the PS because of the constraints of the 24-hour rule, then switched to the more conversational PC. Hortense was not thus constrained, and she actually did the reverse. Over the span of the fours years (1816–20) it took her to compose this journal/memoir, her style became ever more formal (written code). Like her illustrious predecessor, however, whose letters all women of rank had read, she did incorporate some variety into her writing. There was simple narration of events of course, and description of pastoral settings. In addition, she inserted direct quotes from various members of her household and circle of friends. Like Mme de Sévigné who included thoughts attributed to Louis XIV, Hortense included direct and indirect quotes from Napoléon. Unfortunately, the comparison ends there, for Hortense was no Mme de Sévigné. Her writing sounds juvenile to us by contrast. She lacked the literary references and insights of someone who had read widely and critically, and, alas, she lacked the wit and cleverness. There remains the linguistic interest of her words. Her penchant for correctness and obedience gives us an excellent example of the "correct" verb usage of the day. Because she switched from oral to written code, we have reliably correct samples for both for this period.

Cited above are the criteria for what Söll-Hausmann considered to be elements of the "oral code." In addition to use of the PC instead of the PS, he included the repetition of small vocabulary, subjectivity, longer and less profound expression, and verb-orientation—that is, fewer nouns and adjectives. Can these elements be correlated to passages where Hortense uses the PC instead of the PS? There are also the explanations that assign the PS to literary, historical, and "solemn contexts such as births and deaths" (Brill 1983), while the PC is used for events with present relevance, whose effects endure. The former may be simply labeled "written code," while the latter is subsumed as one small element of today's "oral code." Normally, the "oral code" is found in speech and the "written code" is found in printed texts, but not exclusively. Let us consider the four opening paragraphs of the *Mémoires*:

> Ma vie *a été* si brillante et si remplie de malheurs que le
> monde *a dû* s'en occuper. Il m'*a loué*, il m'*a blamée* selon les
> circonstances, mais toujours avec exagération, parce que
> l'élévation de mon rang *a permis* à trop peu de personnes de

m'approcher assez pour me bien juger. Je *crois* n'avoir
mérité ni un éloge trop flatteur, ni une critique trop sévère.
  Mon coeur m'*a* toujours *guidée* dans les moindres démarches
et le coeur *peut*-il tromper quand il est pur? L'enthousiasme
le plus grand pour tout ce qui *est* bien m'*a soutenue* au milieu
des injustices et des revers. Ce sentiment exalté *a fait* sans
cesse ma force et ma consolation.
  C'*est* à quelques âmes élevées et sensibles, à des amis que
je *veux* me faire connaître. J'*entre* dans les plus petits détails
de ma vie en leur *disant*: <Me voilà; *jugez*-moi, *plaignez*-moi,
je *suis* vraie; *aimez*-moi, *estimez*-moi, c'*est* le besoin de mon
coeur, ce *sera* encore le charme de mon existence.> J'*écris*
pour eux seuls.
  Mon frère me *connaît* assez; quelle *est* celle de mes pensées
dont une confiance mutuelle et une vive affection ne l'*aient
rendu* dépositaire? Mes enfants? Ce n'*est* pas de moi qu'ils
doivent apprendre les chagrins que m'*a causés* leur père. J'*ai*
tant *souffert* pour eux, je les *ai* tant *chéris* que, s'ils le *savent*
jamais, ils m'en *aimeront* advantage. Quant à moi, il me *sera*
pénible, sans doute, de retracer les plus belles années de ma
jeunesse passées dans les larmes; mais il y *aura* peut-être de la
douceur à retrouver, parmi les dangers que j'*ai pu* éviter, le peu
de bien que j'*ai pu* faire.

(Mém. 1–2)

  These opening paragraphs exemplify Söll-Hausmann's criteria for the "oral
code," even though they appear within a written text. There is no PS. The verb
forms used are: PC (no longer PC´), IN, P, INP, PPR, IMP, FS, and S. Hortense is addressing her future readers, her friends and family, in what closely
resembles epistolary style. Yes, there is present relevance to her sufferings,
but in the 19th century that was no longer a necessary criterion for PC use,
once the "oral code" had been established. Most of the 14 sentences are superficial and "lengthy." It takes her four paragraphs to explain that she is writing to justify herself, and to reclaim some love and sympathy from her
friends. The paragraphs are verb intensive: there are 18 adjectives (excluding
possessive adjectives), 39 nouns, and 45 verbs. The point of view is subjective: the word "je" appears 9 times, "me" appears 11 times, "ma" appears 5
times, "mes" appears 2 times, and "moi" 6 times. These memoirs are definitely about Hortense, there is no intent to view the world objectively.
  Let us now consider a passage from the middle of the text. Hortense relates
how she mediated a discussion between Napoléon and Joséphine regarding
the latter's eventual residence at Malmaison, after the divorce. The pregnant
Empress Marie-Louise was understandably jealous of her rival, and would

have preferred that Joséphine leave France. According to Hortense, Napoléon
suggested that Hortense could write her mother that he would not oppose
Malmaison as a final retreat. It should be noted that Hanoteau's footnote to
the paperback edition implies that Hortense may have confused a discussion
of Malmaison with a discussion of Navarre (Mém. P.II. 97).

> J'*arrivai* à Fontainebleau où toute la Cour *était* réunie; mes enfants
> m'y *attendaient*. Le soir même, l'Empereur *vint* me voir avec l'Impératrice.
> Il me la *montra* d'un air satisfait: <Voyez comme sa taille *grossit*>,
> me *dit*-il. <Si c'*est* une fille, ce *sera* une petite femme pour votre fils,
> Napoléon, car elle ne *doit* sortir ni de la famille ni de la France, celle-là>.
> Il ne *put* être question de ma mère ce soir-là. Je *demandai* une
> audience pour le lendemain matin et je *devinai* bien, en lui *parlant*, tout
> le plaisir qu'il *aurait eu* à ce que ma mère *choisit* elle-même son séjour
> près de son fils en Italie.
>
> <Je *dois* penser au bonheur de ma femme,> me *dit*-il. <Les
> choses ne se *sont* pas *arrangées* comme je l'*espérais*. Elle *est*
> effarouchée des agréements de votre mère et de l'empire qu'on lui
> *connaît* sur mon esprit. Je le *sais* à n'en pas douter. Dernièrement
> je *voulus* aller me promener avec elle à la Malmaison. J'*ignore* si
> elle *crut* que votre mère y *était,* mais elle se *mit* à pleurer et je *fus*
> *obligé* de changer de direction. Quoi qu'il en *soit*, jamais je ne
> *contraindrai* l'Impératrice Joséphine en rien. Je me *souviendrai*
> toujours du sacrifice qu'elle *a fait*. Si elle *veut* s'établir à Rome,
> je l'en *nommerai* gouvernante. A Bruxelles, elle *peut* encore y
> tenir une Cour superbe et faire meme du bien au pays. Près de
> son fils et de ses petits-enfants, elle *serait* mieux encore et plus
> convenablement. Mais *écrivez*-lui que, si elle *préfère* vivre à
> la Malmaison, je ne m'y *opposerai* pas.> J'*assurai* l'Empereur
> que c'*était* son seul voeu et ma mère *arriva* peu de temps après.
> Je *revins* bientôt répéter de sa part à l'Empereur qu'*ayant été* sa
> femme et Impératrice des Français, elle n'*ambitionnait* plus d'autre
> gloire, qu'elle ne *désirait* que mourir dans sa patrie et au milieu de
> ses amis (Mém. 265–66).

One gets the impression that Hortense occasionally put her own words into
the mouths of people she "quoted." For example, when she quotes Napoléon's
description of his drive to Malmaison with Marie-Louise, Hortense has him
use the PS: "je *voulus* aller me promener. . . J'ignore si elle *crut*. . ." These
words were cited as direct quotations of a conversation, so it is more likely that
Napoléon actually used the PC in both cases, if in fact he actually said those
very words to Hortense. As Hanoteau frequently pointed out in his footnotes,
Hortense occasionally had lapses in memory, or perhaps she embellished a bit.
The unpublished personal letters from Napoléon to Hortense, that form an ap-

pendix toVolume II of the paperback edition of the *Mémoires*, all show PC usage in this form of the oral code. The PS of "je *fus* obligé. . ." is understand-
able, since the PS of "être" was still often substituted for a descriptive I at that
time. The narrative portions of this excerpt generally follow the guidelines for
written code. The PS is used instead of the PC, and the tone is less subjective
than that of the previous passage cited—there are far fewer references to the
first person. The passage is still verb-intensive, however the expression is
more succinct. There are few adjectives.

The final four paragraphs of the *Mémoires* are further evidence of the
shifts between the oral code and the written code. When she addresses her
audience directly, quotes her own thoughts, or cites banal general truths,
Hortense uses the P, FS, I, or PC. When she narrates past events she uses the
PS, PQP, and I:

> Je m'*arrête* ici, je n'*ai* plus rien à raconter; je *puis* revenir sur ma
> vie: elle ne me *fait* plus de mal.
> Tout entière à mes devoirs, envers un époux, j'*avais espéré*
> trouver ma félicité dans un doux intérieur. Je *fus*, hélas! bien
> trompée. Je me *rejetai* sur la véritable affection; je *crus* que, pour
> être heureuse, il *suffisait* d'être aimée, que les sentiments purs et
> tendres *devaient* seuls embellir l'existence: je m'*abusai* encore.
> La perfection n'*est* pas dans le coeur de l'homme, et je *tenais* sans
> cesse à l'y trouver. La bienveillance du monde me *parut* quelques
> instants une compensation; elle *vint* à me manquer aussi, et je
> *cherche* à fortifier mon coeur contre ce nouveau coup. J'*ai* trop
> *compté* sur la perfection humaine, me *disais*-je. Désormais, je
> *ferai* le bien sans rien attendre de personne. Désabusée de tout, je
> *cherche* à me créer un autre bonheur.
> J'*aimerai* mes semblables, je leur *ferai* du bien, mais sans en rien
> attendre: j'*ai* trop *compté* sur eux. Le malheur, la douleur m'*attireront*
> toujours, et, si je *parviens* à les adoucir, je me *dirai*: voilà la véritable
> jouissance, celle que personne n'*aura* le pouvoir de m'enlever.
> Je *crois* donc *avoir trouvé* la véritable route du repos et j'*entre*
> dans l'avenir avec sécurité. Isolée comme je suis, exilée de ma patrie,
> gémissant sur le sort affreux du bienfaiteur de ma famille [Napoléon],
> je me *dis* souvent: <Ma vie *est* pourtant terminée; je ne *crains* plus
> les passions, j'*ai pu* trouver ce qui *calme* et ce qui *rend* meilleur, que
> me *reste*-t-il à désirer pour moi? De *vivre* un peu dans le souvenir
> de mes chers compatriotes, dans le coeur de mes amis, et de *mourir*
> dans les bras de mes enfants: voilà mon dernier voeu.
> (Signed and dated: Augsbourg 1820 hortense [sic]) (Mém. 525–526)

Despite the dramatic allusion to "last wishes" at the end of her journal,
Hortense was to live another seventeen years. One striking element of the oral

code, as laid out by Söll-Hausmann, is evident in these final paragraphs—
"the repetition of small vocabulary." Some of the repeated words or phrases
include: "J'ai trop compté sur," or its near equivalent "Je tenais . . . à," "véri-
table," "le coeur," "je m'abusais" or the reverse "Désabusée," "la perfection,"
and of course "ma vie." When she spoke of the world's opinion in the opening paragraphs, Hortense used the PC ("Le monde m'*a blamée*, "etc.). In the
final paragraphs, the world's judgement is delivered in the PS ("La bienveil-
lance du monde me *parut* . . . elle *vint* à me manquer. . ."). This may indicate
the general shift towards the written code as the *Mémoires* progress, or simply that Hortense was establishing some literary distance from the world's
opinions.

The 19th century saw a rise in usage of the "picturesque imperfect" as an
alternative to the PC or PS. This use of I was already evident in the letters of
Mme de Sévigné, but it seemed to be at its peak at the time of the writings of
Hortense. The use of I may have provided a way of avoiding PC/PS choice,
or it may have been a matter of style. Let us consider the following passage
where Hortense describes the return of Napoléon from his first exile on the
island of Elbe. She had been asked to come to the Tuileries to meet him:

> Un officier de la Garde nationale *vint* à 7 heures du soir, de la part
> des anciens ministres, m'engager à me rendre aux Tuileries pour y
> attendre l'Empereur. Le peuple *entourait* le palais. La vue de ma
> voiture *excita* de vives acclamations. Le poste de la Garde nationale
> de service *prit* les armes à mon arrive et *poussa* de tels cris que je
> *crus* que l'Empereur entrait par une autre porte. Mais, reconnaissant
> bientôt que c'était pour moi, je *souris* à la pensée que, quelques jours
> avant, je *passais* dans ces mêmes lieux inaperçue des hommes qui en
> *faisaient* la garde. Que de différence en un instant! (Mém. 404)

This passage exemplifies narration in the "written code." There is no PC,
only PS and I. The tone is fairly objective, almost that of an "on the scene" re-
porter. The I of "je passais" is of interest here. Because we know that Hortense
had disguised herself to slip by the sentries, in order to leave her residence un-
detected by anxious monarchists, we know that this event represented "punctual aspect." This was not a habitual or repeated event, the normal domains of
I. This use of I is thus a colorful way to avoid using the PA ("fus passée"). The
tone at the end of the paragraph had shifted from objective narrative reporting
to personal observation. However, as long as there was a PS ("souris") in the
preceding clause, Hortense could not have used the more common "oral code"
PQP to express anteriority. Thus the use of I. "The decline of the past definite
[PS] in the spoken language naturally carried with it the decline of the past anterior [PA]" (Richard 116). It may have even preceded it.

5. NAPOLÉON'S LETTERS TO HORTENSE

A selection of previously unpublished letters from Napoléon to Hortense appears at the end of Volumes I and II of Hanoteau's green paperback edition. The content is the typical father (or in this case stepfather)-daughter exchange: discussion of allowances and other expenses, arrangements for visits and travels, and arrangements for Hortense's two sons, Napoléon-Louis [le grand-duc de Berg], age 6, and Charles-Louis Napoléon [future Napoléon III], age 2. Her son Napoléon-Charles had died in 1807 at age 4 1/2. The letter of July 19, 1810 is typical:

> Ma Fille,
>   J'ai reçu votre lettre du 15. J'ai reçu aussi la note sur M. de Spaen.
> Je l'ai fait inscrire comme candidat. Je ne vois plus d'inconvénient
> que vous alliez à Aix. Cela fera plaisir à l'Impératrice qui a, je crois,
> le projet de passer quelque temps à Genève après les eaux.
>   J'attends Napoléon demain ici. Je ne sais pas où est le Roi
> [Hortense's husband Louis]. Soyez bien persuadée que sa
> conduite ne m'inspire pas d'autre sentiment que la pitié.
>   Votre bien affectionné père,
>   NAPOLÉON (sic)
> (A Saint-Cloud, le 19 juillet 1810)   (Mém. P.II, 377–78)

This letter, like the others, is written using the "oral code" of informal speech. Thus, the past is rendered in the PC exclusively. In most of the letters Hortense is addressed as "daughter," but the later letters address her as "sister." Since she married his brother, Hortense is Napoléon's sister-in-law as well as his stepdaughter. He refers to her sons as his "nephews." He nevertheless addresses her with the formal "vous."

6. CONCLUSIONS

By the 19th century it was no longer necessary to establish present relevance or even that the past event was recent in order to use the PC in speech, or in speechlike discourse. In the "oral code" the PC could be used to narrate both recent and historical past events. It thus performed, and still does, the functions of both the present perfect and the preterite in "speech." The PS was, and still is, the past tense of choice of the "written code," that is primarily literary and historical narration. There are interesting exceptions to this. In the mid-1960's a middle-aged French grammar professor at the University of Bordeaux painstakingly explained to the American study-abroad students how the PC and

PS could be used in the same context—oral or written. His argument was based on the old requirement of present relevance, rather than on discourse type. He told a story about threading a needle, the drawing in and out of the thread, and the completed repair on a sock to illustrate how the PS should be used for the entirely past threading ("un temps entièrement évolué") and the repeated ins and outs of hand sewing (punctual aspect), as opposed to the completed repair expressed with a PC (perfective aspect with present relevance). We bought his argument, but noticed that most everyone else never used the PS when they spoke. Many "older" professors in southern France apparently still do.

There are other "oral code" occasions when the PS is not only seen in writing, but also heard in speech. As my previously cited personal letter corpus research showed (Brill 1983:124), there is a tendency to switch to the PS for solemn occasions such as the announcement of births and deaths, even in the middle of a chatty "oral code" letter where most past tense verbs are in the PC. The PS still can lend an air of *gravitas* to the discussion of such events. Likewise, the PS is still seen today in certain newspaper stories, especially in the fast-paced sports stories of newspapers. Newspapers seem to include both "literary" and "oral code" pieces. The sports stories are not generally literary, but something about the short, rapid-fire nuance of the PS is attractive to many sportswriters. And in fact, that story of "the needle" included the key series of three (pulling in and out) that constituted one element of the old PS prescription.

And then there is the recent retirement letter from a distinguished professor of French in the United States, to a leading French journal. How do we explain to our students that this letter, following exactly the prescriptive rules of the "needle story," reflects perfect 17th to 19th century French? The archaic sounding PS ("nous mîmes") would have made Charles Perrault proud.

BIBLIOGRAPHY

Hanlet, L'Abbé C. *Introduction aux Lettres de Mme de Sévigné*. Bruxelles: Anc. Établiss. J. Lebègue & Cie, 1945.

Hoffmann, Léon-François. *Le Nègre romantique: personnage littéraire et obsession collective*. Paris: Payot, 1973.

Mémoires de la Reine Hortense. Pub. par le Prince Napoléon avec notes de Jean. Hanoteau. Tome Premier, 16e éd. Paris: Plon, 1927.

Mémoires de la Reine Hortense. Pub. par le Prince Napoléon avec notes de Jean Hanoteau. Tome Deuxième, 5e éd. Paris: Plon, 1927.

Mémoires de la Reine Hortense. Pub. par le Prince Napoléon avec notes de Jean Hanoteau. Édition Illustrée (en un grand volume rouge). Paris: Plon, 1927.

Söll, Ludwig. *Gesprochene und geschriebene Französisch*. 1974. Rev. ed. by Franz Joseph Hausmann. Berlin: Erich Schmidt Verlag, 1980.

Ziolkowski, Jan, ed. *On Philology*. University Park and London: The Pennsylvania State University Press, 1990.

Appendix

Fairy tales have always been narrated in the PS. The tradition endures today whether the tales are recited aloud or read from a book. Sometimes, however, the tale is told in the timeless present. The reason for both usages is simple. Children and adults who have heard a tale repeatedly, tend to retell it almost exactly as they heard it. Even when descriptive details, or even storylines are altered in the retelling, the verb forms tend to remain the same.

The following three versions of *Le Petit Chaperon Rouge* were recorded near La Rochelle, France in 1980 by a then fellow graduate student visiting his French in-laws. They were told that a friend of his was researching versions of fairy tales. Of course, I was also listening to their verb usage. The recordings were made with a microphone and an old portable cassette tape recorder. The participants were a mother, a daughter, and a visiting family friend.

1. MALE, AGE 60+

Il était une fois, dans la maison des bois, une mignonne petite fille qui aimait bien son papa et sa maman. Sa maman la nourissait très bien, l'habillait très joliment, et avait toujours soin qu'elle soit bien lavée et bien brossée. Quand sa maman voulait que sa fille s'en aille dehors pour le jeu, elle lui mettait sur la tête un petit chaperon tout rouge, de façon que tous les gens qui rencontraient cette petite fille l'appelaient toujours «le Petit Chaperon Rouge.»

Un matin la maman du Petit Chaperon Rouge lui dit: «Il fait longtemps que tu n'as pas apporté de provisions à ta mère-grand! Il faut que tu y ailles pour qu'elle ait au moment de son déjeuner une bonne écuelle de beurre, les cinq galettes qu'elle aime tant, et des pommes de notre fruitier. Je vais te les mettre dans un panier. Pendant ce temps, va mettre ton chaperon rouge!»

47

Le Petit Chaperon Rouge alla s'habiller, et quand elle revint, elle trouva le panier tout prêt, qu'elle suspendit à son cou de gauche. Au moment de passer la porte de la maison des bois, sa maman lui dit: «Attention, Petit Chaperon Rouge! Prends le grand chemin, ne va pas à travers les broussailles! Bien sûr, dans les broussailles tu feras beaucoup de belles découvertes, mais dans les broussailles le grand loup pourrait te sentir! Il pourrait renifler avec son grand nez que tu as une délicieuse chair, bon à manger, et alors il te sauterait dessus et il te mangerait! Alors, garde le grand chemin! Et sur le grand chemin ne parle à personne! On ne sait pas qui peut se déguiser.»

Le Petit Chaperon Rouge fit toutes les promesses que sa maman lui demandait et prit la route guillemettement [guillerettement]. Pendant qu'elle était sur le grand chemin, justement, le loup arrive:

«Mmm!» dit le loup.
«Mmmmm!» dit le loup.

Mais le Petit Chaperon Rouge était sur le grand chemin, il savait [que] sur le grand chemin il n'avait pas de danger, sauf si on parlait à des gens, mais le loup n'était pas un gens. Et justement le loup lui parle:

«Où vas-tu comme ça Petit Chaperon Rouge?»
«Je vais chez ma mère-grand.»
«Mais qu'est-ce que tu vas faire chez ta mère-grand?»
«Je vais lui apporter son déjeuner.»
«Qu'est-ce qu'il y a dans son déjeuner?»
«Tu vois, dans mon panier il y a des galettes, et il y a des pommes de notre fruitier.»
«Ah, elle sera bien contente, ta mère-grand.»
«Ah, oui!»
«Et, où est-ce qu'elle habite ta mère-grand?»
«Ah, elle habite de l'autre côté du champs de blé noir, dans la maison qui fume toujours.»
«Ah, je vois,» dit le loup. «Et bien, bonne route, Petit Chaperon Rouge. Au revoir!»
«Au revoir, monsieur le loup!»

Et le loup s'en alla à grand galop à travers les allées. Et le Petit Chaperon Rouge continua son chemin et [ne] rencontra personne. Il n'y eut pas de gens qui lui parlassent et auxquelles elle fut obligée de ne pas répondre. Et elle arrive à la maison de chaume de l'autre côté du champs de blé noir.

«Toc, toc, toc,» elle frappe.

Et du fond de la maison on entend une grosse voix. Que veut cette voix? La grand-mère dit:

«Qui est là?»
«C'est ta petite fille, le Petit Chaperon Rouge. Veux-tu m'ouvrir mère-grand?»
«Non, je ne veux pas t'ouvrir, je suis au fond de mon lit.»
«Ah, c'est pour ça que tu as une si grosse voix, mère-grand? Tu as attrapé le rhume peut-être?»
«Oh, oui, j'ai attrapé le rhume, même pire que ça.»
«Mais alors, comment je vais faire ce pour entrer?»
«Oh, ne t'inquiète pas ! Appuie sur la chevillette, et la targette cherrera [cherra]!»

Le Petit Chaperon Rouge appuya sur la chevillette, et la targette chut. La porte s'ouvrit, et la petite fille entra. La maison était un petit peu noire, parce que c'était une maison d'autrefois pour les mères-grand. Elles [ne] peuvent pas beaucoup supporter la lumière à cause de leurs vieux yeux. Alors, elle [ne] voyait pas très bien, mais elle voyait bien dans le grand lit là au fond de la salle le grand bonnet blanc de nuit de sa mère-grand, et le casaquin [casaque] de sa mère-grand. Les doigts et le nez étaient cachés sous les couvertures. Et le Petit Poucet [Petit Chaperon Rouge] était là à la regarder, et du fond du lit la voix revient:

«Avance donc, Petit Chaperon Rouge! Il faut que je t'embrasse!»

Le Petit Chaperon Rouge fait quelques pas, puis hésite, tant c'était curieux. Ça avait un drôle d'odeur! La mère-grand:

«Mais Petit Chaperon Rouge, qu'est-ce qui te fait hésiter? Oh, mais je vois que tu as un panier pendu à ton cou de gauche. Qu'est-ce qu'i[l] y a dans ton panier?»
«Ah, dans mon panier il y a des choses pour toi mère-grand. Il y a une pleine écuelle de beurre, et il y a des galettes que tu aimes tant, et il y a des pommes de notre fruitier pour ton déjeuner.»
«Mon Petit Chaperon Rouge, tu es bien gentil. Alors, viens ici que je t'embrasse!»

Le Petit Chaperon Rouge avança, posa sur la table son panier, et alla jusqu'au lit pour embrasser la mère-grand. Et là, elle fut étonnée:

«Mère-grand, je comprends bien que tu es enrhumée, et que tu aies une voix si grave et si basse, mais comment ce fait-il que tu as un si grand nez?»

«J'ai un si grand nez pour mieux sentir la bonne odeur de la viande fraîche.»
«Mère-grand, ce n'est pas de la viande fraîche que je t'apporte, c'est du beurre
et des galettes, et des pommes de notre fruitier.»
«Mais, il y a une autre viande fraîche que je sens!»

Et comme elle parlait la [le] Petit Chaperon Rouge vit des grandes dents dans
sa bouche.

«Oh, mais regarde comme tu as des grandes dents. Je ne savais pas que tu avais
de si grandes dents.»
«Mais si j'ai des grandes dents, c'est pour mieux manger la viande fraîche.
Alors, viens m'embrasser!»

Et le Petit Chaperon Rouge s'avança pour embrasser la mère-grand, et à ce
moment-là bondit le grand loup qui avait mis les habits et la coiffe de la mère-
grand. Avec ses pattes il embrassa le Petit Chaperon Rouge, et avec ses
grandes dents elle s'est mis à le croquer, non, il s'est mis à la croquer. Et le
pauvre Petit Chaperon Rouge fut mangé par le grand loup, parce qu'il n'avait
pas compris que quand on dit «les gens,» ce n'est pas seulement des hommes,
mais c'est même des animaux.

Comments

This informant tells the most complete and amusing version of the tale. He uses
mainly the PS to narrate, but occasionally lapses into historic P. Of linguistic interest is the occasional dropping of "l" in "il," and the deletion of the negative
particle "ne." Both of these deletions are signs of the oral code. Of particular interest is the thorny problem of gender reference when the natural gender of the
protagonist differs from the name of that character. Whereas the little girl is
clearly female, her name in French is masculine, because the word for "hood" is
masculine. Similar issues arise in such fairy tales as *Bluebeard*, where the main
character is male, but the word for "beard" is feminine in French, and *Beauty
and the Beast*, where the word for "beast" is feminine in French. In a presenta-
tion to the Kentucky Philological Association in 1997, I noted that male authors
such as Charles Perrault generally used, "sylleptic" agreement (agreement with
the natural gender). Thus Perrault referred to the title character of "Le Petit
Chaperon Rouge" as "elle," and the character "La Barbe Bleue" was referred to
as "il." Madame LePrince de Beaumont did the reverse in writing *La Belle et la
Bête*. She observed proper grammatical agreement in most cases, but often alternated the feminine word "beast," with the masculine word "monster." When
Jean Cocteau filmed this classic tale in 1946, he also regularly alternated the
words "beast" and "monster" in the script. He could thus use a masculine refer-

ential pronoun when necessary, which probably sounded more natural to film audiences. Like de Beaumont, however, Cocteau often chose to use "elle" the feminine pronoun when referring to the clearly male beast. This was more in line with his famous penchant for playing with gender identity, and perhaps an allusion to his own homosexuality. English translations of the film could neutralize this wordplay. There is one interesting instance in the film when the French "elle" (for the beast) simply appears as "he" in the English subtitles.

This narrator generally observes grammatical agreement, but lapses into sylleptic error, toward the end, as in "Et comme *elle* parlait *la* Petit Chaperon Rouge vit des grandes dents. . ." It would be permissible to use a feminine pronoun to refer to the character, but never a feminine article with a masculine noun and adjective. There is momentary gender breakdown at the end as well, possibly due to the confusing contradiction of the girl's French name and her natural gender, when he states that "she ate him," "no, he ate her." Both of these "performance" errors are typical of the oral code. The grammatically correct statement would have been "he ate him" (referring to *le* Petit Chaperon Rouge). This is not only ambiguous, but sounds odd, so the eventual choice of sylleptic agreement worked best: "il s'est mis à la croquer" 'he started to eat her.'

2. A MOTHER, AGE 40+

Il était une fois un Petit Chaperon Rouge, à qui sa maman avait tricoté un joli petit bonnet de laine, tout rouge. Elle était si mignon . . . il était si mignon . . . c'était une petite fille un peu désobéissante, mais si mignonne que quand sa maman lui dit:

> «Va voir ta mère-grand, je n'ai pas eu le temps ces jours-ci, mais tu serais bien gentille d'aller lui porter cette galette et ce pot de beurre que j'ai préparé pour elle. Alors, tu mets ton petit chaperon et tu pars. Seulement, fais bien attention, ça n'est pas bien loin, mais il faut traverser un peu de la forêt, et tu risques de rencontrer le loup. Alors, écoute-moi bien, tu marches vite, tu te dépêches un peu, et puis de toute façon tu dois revenir assez vite. En même temps tu me diras comment va ta grand-mère.»

Alors, le Petit Chaperon Rouge part, son petit panier au bras, toute contente et toute guillerette, traverse le village, puis se trouve dans . . . dans la forêt. Là, elle regarde un peu à droite à gauche . . . euh . . . elle oublie déjà ce que lui a dit sa maman. Ça sent bon. Il y a des (sic) petites fleurs. C'est . . . c'est bien agréable. Et puis, après tout, qui peut-elle rencontrer? Elle prend son temps.

Mais, au detour du . . . d'un chemin elle aperçoit le loup. Elle a d'abord un peu peur, mais le loup se fait tout gentil, s'approche d'elle et lui dit:

«Où vas-tu ma mignonne?»
«Eh bien, je vais porter cette galette et ce pot de beurre chez ma mère-grand. Maman . . . euh . . . c'est maman qui m'envoie.»
«Ah, mais ta mère-grand, tu . . . elle . . . elle est loin d'ici?»
«Non, non, du tout, à la sortie du bois, la première maison, dès que commence le village.»
«Ah, très bien, très bien. Eh bien, bonne journée petite fille. Amuse-toi bien!"

Et le loup s'en va vite. Lui, les jambes à son cou, il n'a pas une minute à perdre, certainement. Il semble très pressé. La petite fille continue. Elle cueille . . . un bouquet, un bouquet de petites fleurs, elle voit deux ou trois champignons, elle ramasse des (sic) petites plumes d'oiseaux, elle met tout ça dans son panier, et elle est toute contente, et puis tout d'un coup elle se dit:

«Oh, quand même, que je me dépêche!»

Et elle part. Et elle arrive à la maison de sa grand-mère. Euh, les volets sont tirés, et la porte est fermée, mais elle reconnaît bien le loquet habituel. Euh, elle est toute mignonne, euh, elle est quand même un peu inquiète de voir cette maison fermée. Elle frappe d'abord. Habituellement sa grand-mère est là sur le seuil de la porte. Elle vient lui ouvrir. Alors, elle frappe, et elle entend, euh, une voix lui répondre:

«Qui est là?»

Une voix qu'elle ne reconnaît pas très bien d'abord. Alors, elle frappe une seconde fois:

«Toc, toc!»
«Qui est là?»
«C'est votre petite fille, le Petit Chaperon Rouge. Ma mère m'envoie vous porter une galette et un pot de beurre.»
«Ah, ma bonne petite! Entre, entre! Je . . . entre, je ne me dérange pas, je suis un peu enrhumée, et aujourd'hui je resterai au lit.»

La petite fille fait ce que lui dit sa grand-mère. Sa grand-mère lui dit . . . mais:

«Mais tu sais bien qu'il y a la chevillette, la bobinette cherra.»
«Ah, oui, oui, mère-grand, c'est vrai.»

Alors, elle tire la chevillette et la porte s'ouvre, et elle rentre dans la cuisine de sa grand-mère. Elle aperçoit son bonnet de nuit tout blanc. Elle voit aussi le gros édredon qu'on fait de plumes. Elle est un peu douteuse. Sa grand-mère est malade. Alors, elle s'approche de sa grand-mère pour lui dire bonjour, et elle trouve quand même sa grand-mère un peu bizarre ce matin. Elle n'avait pas la même voix que d'habitude. Puis, elle est cachée, cachée sous son édredon. Un peu inquiète elle lui dit:

«Oh, mère-grand, mais vous êtes très enrhumée! Vous avez un drôle de voix!»
«Mais, c'est pour mieux te parler, mon enfant.»
«Mère-grand, que vous avez un grand nez!»
«C'est pour mieux sentir, mon enfant.»
«Mère-grand, que vous avez de grandes oreilles!»
« C'est pour mieux t'entendre, mon enfant.»
«Mais mère-grand, que vous avez de grandes dents!»»
«C'est pour mieux te manger!»

Et là-dessus, la mère-grand saute sur le Petit Chaperon Rouge, et n'en fait qu'une bouchée. C'est l'histoire d'une petite fille désobéissante.

Comments

At the end of her taped segment the mother states that it was not a terrific telling, that there were "breakdowns." The male subject, who had been allowed to sit in after he had finished his version, remarked to the mother that she had left out the whole segment where the wolf comes to the grandmother's house. The mother agreed that this was an omission on her part.

This subject had more trouble with the "grammatical versus sylleptic" gender agreement issue than the previous subject. It is likely that she remembered the adjective "mignon" in its masculine form from versions she had previously heard. She solved the problem by restating that "Little Red Riding Hood" was a girl. She then proceeded to use feminine agreement. There were a few "performance" errors, and other examples of the oral code: hesitations, repetitions, self-correction via reformulation of a thought, and some inconsistency in vocabulary. The latter was most evident in the switching between "mère-grand," and "grand-mère." "Mère-grand, the traditional archaic form for "grandmother," most used in fairy tales, was generally used in the dialogue portions, which probably came word for word from memory.

The mother used only the historic present in the narrative portions of this tale. On the face of it this could be considered a disappointing result for the purposes of this study. However, when prompted by my friend to tell the story in the past, the mother explained that she could only tell it in the present, because

that is how she had learned it. This reinforces my earlier claim that the essen-
tial elements of fairy tales, especially including their verb forms, are handed
down in mostly memorized chunks of language. Others have made this observation about tales in general, but the emphasis here is that verb forms are also
handed down as they were previously heard.

3. A DAUGHTER, AGE 20+

Il était une fois le Petit Chaperon Rouge. Euh, . . . le Petit Chaperon Rouge
avait . . . euh . . . non! La grand-mère du Petit Chaperon Rouge était malade.
Sa maman lui dit:

> «Va amener (sic) des provisions à ta grand-mère!»

Elle lui donne un tas de paniers avec beaucoup de choses très bonnes pour
sa santé. Des suisses [fam. fromage petit-suisse] douces, et des oranges, des
jus de fruits, enfin un tas de choses. La petite fille s'en va toute guillerette au
chaumet [chaumière] de sa grand-mère avec le panier. En forêt elle rencontre
le loup. Le loup, très aimable, approche (sic) la petite fille et lui dit:

> «Que vas-tu faire?»
> «Je vais voir ma grand-mère.»
> «Ah, bon? Et ta grand-mère, comment va-t-elle?»
> «Elle est malade. Je lui amène (sic) un tas de provisions.»
> «Ah, eh bien, je vais aller la voir, moi aussi.»

Le loup s'en va, bien avant la petite fille, et va sonner chez la grand-mère.
La grand-mère, inquiète, dit:

> «Qui est là?»

Le loup répond sur le ton de la petite fille:

> «C'est moi!»
> «Ouvre, ouvre! la bobinette cherra,» dit la grand-mère.

Le loup entre. La grand-mère lui demande ce qu'il vient faire. Mais le loup
est déguisé en petite fille, elle ne le reconnaît pas. Le loup lui dit:

> «Oh, grand-mère, que tu as un grand nez!»

Et elle lui répond:

«C'est pour mieux te sentir, mon enfant.»
«Oh, grand-mère, que tu as de grandes oreilles aujourd'hui!»
«C'est pour mieux t'entendre, mon enfant.»
«Oh, grand-mère, euh . . ., que tu as une grande bouche!»
«Oh, grand-mère, que tu as de grandes dents!»

Et le loup mange la grand-mère.

Pendant ce temps, la petite fille continue sa promenade, et elle arrive chez la grand-mère. Elle frappe, comme d'ordinaire, et le loup, imitant la grand-mère, lui dit:

«Entre, mon enfant!»

La petite fille entre avec son panier, et voit sa grand-mère dans son lit. Elle lui dit:

«Comment vas-tu, grand-mère?»

La grand-mère lui répond:

«Je vais bien.»

Et là, elle dit la même chose que le loup:

«Oh, grand-mère, que tu as un grand nez aujourd'hui!»
«C'est pour mieux te sentir, mon enfant.»
«Oh, grand-mère, que tu as de grandes oreilles!»
«C'est pour mieux t'entendre, mon enfant.»
«Oh, grand-mère, que tu as de grandes dents, aujourd'hui!»
«C'est pour mieux te manger, mon enfant!»

Et le loup abat la petite fille.

Comments

Like her mother, this female subject recounts this tale in the historic present. There is obvious confusion in the scene where the wolf first confronts the grandmother. The girl knows the traditional set of memorized questions, but first attributes them to the wolf, disguised as a little girl. In what must be considered a simple "performance error," she conflates the arrival scenes of the wolf and Little Red Riding Hood. Thus we have the odd questioning of the grandmother by the wolf, dressed as a little girl. It is the wolf who asks the grandmother about her big nose, ears, and teeth. This is really funny, and one can hear the tittering in the background on the tape recording. The teller

recovers, after some hesitation, by simply stating that the wolf ate the grandmother. She must have realized that she had made a mistake, but she went
on. This is one example of how oral tales can be modified over the years. The
"mistake" also serves to support the idea that tales are told in memorized
"chunks" of language.

This version is the briefest of the three. The daughter uses informal, often
familiar, language, and never uses the archaic fairy tale "mère-grand" for
"grandmother." She obviously knew the general outline of the story, and she
copied her mother's verb usage, but she was a little rusty on the details. Instead of a basket of cakes, butter, and apples, she speaks of baskets of sweet
cheese, oranges, and fruit juices—probably a reflection of her own dietary
choices.

Index

Plautus, vii

Prince Napoléon, 32

register, 10

Saracens, 1, 3, 7, 31

secrets and language choice, 5

slavery, 34, 35, 38, 39

social class: and education, 22, 37, 40;
    and manners, 19, 20; and personal

pronouns, 38, 45; and the Revolution,
    35, 36; and skin color, 34, 35; and
    verb choice, 3, 8, 10, 12, 13, 14, 29

subjectivity: and FC, 28; and PC, 40, 41

theatre: eighteenth century French, 35;
    puppet, 4, 5, 12; seventeenth century
    French, 21; street, 4, 5

written code, 22, 32, 33, 40, 43, 44, 45